Praise for *Building Natural Ponds*

I love "all things water," and I was thrilled to read the most comprehensive book on designing and building natural ponds. Pavlis has provided detailed, step-by-step instructions about all aspects of ponds. He even discusses large dams, rain gardens, bog gardens, maintenance and much more. What intrigued me was ways to build ponds that did not require any pumps or filtration, and could be set up by anyone with basic skills in shaping soil, placing stone and planting. A must-read for the garden enthusiast and designer.

— Dr. Ross Mars, Permaculture Elder and author,
The Permaculture Transition Manual
and *The Basics of Permaculture Design*

I've never put in a pond, but after reading Robert Pavlis' *Building Natural Ponds*, I am confident that I could do it. And, after reading the book, I will! The book is very thorough, with guidance for every step from planning to digging to stocking with fish to planting to…well, everything you need to know.

— Lee Reich, PhD, author, *The Pruning Book,*
Uncommon Fruits for Every Garden
and *Landscaping with Fruit*
www.leereich.com

Build your own "golden pond" with this complete, authoritative and wonderfully illustrated guide. Robert Pavlis has a knack for making a complex, natural ecosystem seem both straightforward and accessible. *Building Natural Ponds* is the perfect book for anyone who wants a pond, or is eager to improve the one they already have by making it a healthy, functioning ecosystem without any pumps, pipes, chemicals—or algae. From small ponds to large, with a plethora of plant options and covering everything from planning and designing to construction, *Building Natural Ponds* covers it all. Pavlis is just the right person to lead us to some water in our backyards or on our homesteads.

— John D. Ivanko, co-author,
Rural Renaissance and *ECOpreneuring*

There are many reasons to add a water feature to the landscape. Whether it's a tranquil stone lined goldfish pool, or a larger pond for swimming, fishing and irrigation, a pond can greatly increase the biodiversity and beauty of a landscape. They can help manage storm water and provide harvests of food and craft materials. *Building Natural Ponds* is a detailed guide to planning, designing and building ponds, enhancing both your landscape and your life with open water.

— Darrell E. Frey, Three Sisters Farm, author,
Bioshelter Market Garden
and *The Food Forest Handbook*

I've always warned gardeners that a pond, however wonderful for its contribution, will be the most maintenance-demanding aspect of the landscape. The dream is to create a balanced miniature ecosystem in which you don't need massive pumps and filters—after all, there aren't any such machines in a natural pond. How can that dream be realized? With nature's help, Robert Pavlis shows us how.

— Ken Druse, award-winning author
www.KenDruse.com

As someone who has struggled with an assortment of pond challenges over the past 15 years, I can say with certainty that this is the book that every pond owner or wanna-be needs to read. It's always wonderful to come across an author who, like me, ignored all the people who said something couldn't be done—and learned how to do it!

— Deborah Niemann, author,
Homegrown and Handmade,
Ecothrifty, and *Raising Goats Naturally*

BUILDING
Natural Ponds

BUILDING
Natural Ponds

Create a Clean, Algae-free Pond
without Pumps, Filters, or Chemicals

ROBERT PAVLIS

new society
PUBLISHERS

Cover design by Diane McIntosh.
Central pond image: author supplied; all others © iStock.
All interior images ©Robert Pavlis unless otherwise noted.

Funded by the Government of Canada	Financé par le gouvernement du Canada	Canada

Printed in Canada. Third printing June 2020.

Inquiries regarding requests to reprint all or part of *Building Natural Ponds* should be addressed to New Society Publishers at the address below.
To order directly from the publishers, please call toll-free (North America) 1-800-567-6772, or order online at www.newsociety.com

Any other inquiries can be directed by mail to:

New Society Publishers
P.O. Box 189, Gabriola Island, BC V0R 1X0, Canada
(250) 247-9737

LIBRARY AND ARCHIVES CANADA CATALOGUING IN PUBLICATION

Pavlis, Robert, 1953–, author
Building natural ponds : create a clean, algae-free pond without pumps, filters, or chemicals / Robert Pavlis.

Includes bibliographical references and index.
Issued in print and electronic formats.
ISBN 978-0-86571-845-6 (softcover).—ISBN 978-1-55092-640-8 (PDF).—
ISBN 978-1-77142-235-2 (HTML)

1. Ponds—Design and construction.   2. Water in landscape architecture.
I. Title.

| SB475.8.P38 2017 | 714 | C2017-900413-1 |
| | | C2017-900414-X |

New Society Publishers' mission is to publish books that contribute in fundamental ways to building an ecologically sustainable and just society, and to do so with the least possible impact on the environment, in a manner that models this vision.

Dedicated to my wife, Judy,
who has always stood by me while I explore crazy ideas.
This book would not be possible without her support.

Contents

Introduction

I have always wanted a larger pond in my new garden, and it was time to plan for it. It would be located at the top of a hill, next to a wooded area. This is a very natural area that has not been cultivated for many years. The design of the new pond had to fit into this environment and look as old as the mature trees and shrubs around it.

Pond building was not entirely new to me. I had built a few small traditional ponds in the past, and my last project was a large, multi-level waterfall and pond combination. These had all followed traditional designs and used pumps to keep the water clean. My new pond would be in an area that did not have electricity, and I didn't really want to run a new electric line to the location. I wondered, is it possible to build a pond with no electricity?

Why not just build a pond, fill it with water, and let nature take care of things? That seemed like a simple solution to the electricity problem. After much research in books and online, one point became very clear. Everybody agreed on one thing. A natural lined pond without pumps and filters would never work. In no time at all, it would become an algae cesspool of stinking organic matter. These so-called experts gave some vague reasons why it would not work, but nobody said that they had actually tried it.

My background is in chemistry and biology, and I have been studying plants and gardening all my life. I understood water chemistry, and the biology of water life. I maintained aquariums and bred fish for over ten years. One of my projects was to set up two five-foot long aquariums with no air and no filters. They contained a limited number of fish and lots of plants. All I did was feed the fish and replace some water once a month. After five years, they were still going strong with no water quality problems and no need for chemicals. In that time, they were never dismantled for cleaning. The plants and fish grew so well that I had to remove some every six months. The key to these self-sufficient aquariums was the plants—lots of them. They were my air pump and filter, and they cleaned up the fish poop for me.

Why could I not replicate the self-contained aquariums in a pond? Mother Nature does it all of the time. Everything I knew about ponds, water chemistry, fish, and plants told me that it would work. Everything I read told me it would not.

After a lot of thought, I concluded that the experts must be wrong. I convinced myself that if a pond was designed correctly, following nature's guidelines, it would work. So I set out to prove the experts wrong.

That was eight years ago. Almost from day one, the pond was a success. In the first couple of years, I did have some algae in the pond, but that was because the plants had not yet established themselves. To be honest, I cheaped out and did not buy enough plants. Each year as the plants multiplied, the amount of algae decreased. I'll explain this key relationship later in more detail.

About four years into the project, the water was crystal clear. I could easily see to the bottom of my four-foot-deep pond. Algae were no longer a problem. The plants were healthy. The pond had lots of frogs and other insects. The fish were growing and breeding. I did nothing to maintain the pond—I didn't even feed the fish.

It has now been eight years, and I am totally convinced that man-made ponds can be successful without pumps, filters, and chemicals.

Why did my pond work when all of the experts said it wouldn't? The key is in the design of the pond. If you follow traditional pond designs and just leave out the pumps and filters, they will fail. You will have created a great place to grow algae. In a traditional pond, the pumps and filters play a critical role, and you can't just remove them.

This book will explain how to design the pond to work without equipment and chemicals and why the design works. You will gain a new understanding of natural biological systems and how nature solves the algae problem.

As a garden designer, I always look at such projects on a more holistic basis. It is not just about adding a pond. To look right, the pond has to be part of the whole garden design. That is why I added a section to the book that talks about designing the look and feel of the pond. It is one thing to make the pond function and quite another to have it look natural.

To better understand the characteristics that make a pond look natural, I'll analyze some ponds that are not man-made. I call these "native" ponds to distinguish them from "natural" man-made ponds.

This is not just a how-to book. I am a big believer in understanding the "why." If you know why things work, you will be better equipped to solve problems as they arise. You will also be able to modify the designs to fit your own situation. The chapter on balanced ecosystems will take you back to school and provide essential background that will give you a deep understanding of the life in your pond. Consider it essential reading.

The information in this book will contradict much of what you find in other pond books and websites. In some cases, that other information is just plain wrong and is presented mostly to sell products that are not needed. In other cases, the information will be correct for traditional pond designs but will not apply to my natural designs. I have included a section about some of these issues so that you understand why the discrepancies exist.

Do traditional ponds work? Absolutely. My issue with traditional ponds is that they are not environmentally friendly. Buying expensive equipment that you don't need is not good for the environment. Using electricity when you don't need it is a waste of resources. Adding unnecessary chemicals is just bad for the environment. My natural pond design requires none of the above. Except for some water, it makes no demands on the environment.

I hope you enjoy this book and that you complete your project. A pond is the most enjoyable thing you can add to your garden.

CHAPTER 1

Understanding a Balanced Ecosystem

You are sitting beside your pond, trying to take it all in. A frog chirps at the edge of a lily pad. A dragonfly skims the surface of the water. Two fish chase each other, darting in and out of the plant roots. It is all very peaceful, or at least it seems to be. In reality, the pond is a natural system undergoing continuous changes. Birth, life, and death are constant. Chemical changes are also taking place every second of every day. As large inhabitants of this pond world, we can't see most of these. We only see the bigger things that happen like the jumping frog. What seems like such a simple world is actually very complex. The great thing for us, the pond caretaker, is that nature manages all of this complexity for us. We only need to provide a hole and some water. Nature will take care of the rest, provided that we build the hole in such a way that it allows nature to do her thing. This chapter provides background information on some of the natural processes taking place in a pond.

What is a balanced ecosystem? To understand this better, we should start with the word "ecosystem." An ecosystem is defined as a biological community of interacting organisms and their physical environment. A pond is an ecosystem since it contains a wide range of organisms living both in the water and around the water. Once your pond is established, it will be an ecosystem containing thousands of different species of life-forms. That number may surprise you, but it is certainly true. All of these organisms interact with each other, either directly or indirectly. Each organism has an effect on the others.

The goal for a natural pond is to have a balanced ecosystem, in which there are no major changes. An insect may be eaten, but it is replaced with another. Some organisms die, but as they decompose, they provide life for new organisms. No one single organism becomes so dominant that it takes over the pond. The water chemistry is stable without large variations in pH and oxygen levels. This is important since every organism has a preferred set of environmental conditions. If the pH level changes too much, a specific organism may leave or die. If all of the mosquitoes suddenly die, the frogs have nothing to eat. The heron in turn has to try and survive on skinny frogs. The pond is no longer in balance.

One of the major problems of most ponds is the growth of algae. Some algae is actually good for the pond, but too much causes an imbalance in the ecosystem that in turn leads to other problems. Too much algae is also an aesthetic problem. We don't like looking at it.

A balanced ecosystem will have small amounts of algae present. A combination of other organisms and environmental conditions will keep the algae from taking over the pond. If one of these controlling factors becomes out of balance, the algae will take over the pond. As pond caretakers it is our job to create a pond in such a way that it can become balanced. Once it has reached a balanced state, it is then our job to help nature maintain the balance. A balanced ecosystem will not allow algae to take over the pond.

In order to maintain the balance in the pond, you need to understand the various organisms in the pond as well as the effect of various environmental factors. The rest of this chapter will delve into these matters.

Oxygen Cycle

All animals, including insects, birds, and fish, breathe in oxygen and breathe out carbon dioxide. Animals that live outside of the pond have easy access to oxygen since they can breathe in air. For the animals in the water, it is a bit more complicated. They must get their oxygen by extracting it from the water. Fish, for example, pass water over their gills and extract the oxygen in the process.

The oxygen level in air is fairly constant—it always contains the same amount of oxygen, and we therefore never have a problem breathing except in special situations like a house fire. In a house fire, the burning process creates carbon dioxide. When we breathe in high levels of carbon dioxide, we don't get enough oxygen and we suffocate.

A very similar thing happens to fish. If the oxygen level in water gets too low, they suffocate and die. Living in water is more precarious than living in air since it takes a very small amount of excess carbon dioxide to kill a fish and the amount of oxygen and carbon dioxide in water is constantly changing.

The oxygen level in air is about 200,000 ppm (20 percent), and pond water will seldom have more than 10 ppm. When levels reach 3 ppm, fish will be stressed; at 2 ppm they die. Low oxygen levels are the major cause of fish deaths in ponds. Oxygen levels affect all of the animals living in water the same way, including the ones you can't see like bacteria.

Bacteria also play a critical role in the oxygen cycle. I'll discuss bacteria in more detail below, but for now think of bacteria as having a biology

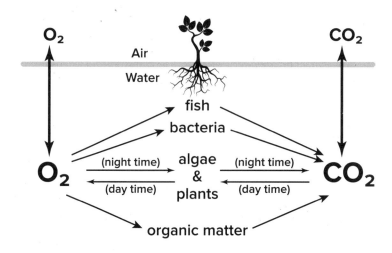

FIGURE 1
Oxygen cycle

similar to humans. They breathe in oxygen, and give off carbon dioxide. Bacteria are vital to maintaining a balanced ecosystem, and their death causes numerous problems for a pond. This is the primary reason for keeping oxygen levels high.

You may be familiar with the fact that plants use carbon dioxide during photosynthesis and give off oxygen. What is not as commonly known is that plant roots absorb oxygen all of the time, even during photosynthesis. Plants that have roots in the water and their leaves outside the water are sucking oxygen out of the water and releasing it into the air, thereby reducing oxygen levels in the water. Even at night when photosynthesis stops, these plants continue to remove oxygen from the water.

Fully submerged plants also affect oxygen levels. During the day, when the sun is shining, these plants will, through photosynthesis, add more oxygen to the water than they take out through their roots. When nighttime comes, the plants stop photosynthesis and stop adding oxygen to the water. But the roots continue using oxygen from the water. The oxygen levels in a pond at night are lower than during the day, and this can be a real problem for animals. If levels fall too low during the night, they may die.

Algae are plants, and they produce oxygen during the day and use up oxygen during the night. This is one of the main reasons that algae levels need to be controlled in a pond. High levels of algae will reduce oxygen levels at night and kill fish, insects, and bacteria.

Temperature also affects oxygen levels. Warm water holds less oxygen than cold water. Warm temperatures also increase fish activity that increases the consumption of oxygen. If it is cloudy, plants photosynthesize less, producing less oxygen. On a warm, cloudy summer day, the fish are active and the water holds less oxygen. This can be the hardest time for fish to get enough oxygen.

In addition to the effects of plants, animals, and temperature, other processes affect the oxygen level in ponds. One of the most significant is the exchange of gases between water and air. At the surface of the pond where the water and air meet, there is a constant exchange of gases.

Oxygen moves from water to air, and from air to water. It is moving in both directions at the same time. When the oxygen levels are low in the water, most of the movement is from air to water, increasing the level of oxygen in the water.

Carbon dioxide is also a gas and does the same thing. It is moving from water to air and back again. When CO_2 levels are high in water, most of the movement is out of the water, resulting in lower CO_2 levels in the water.

This exchange of gases happens all of the time, night and day, and is critical for maintaining balanced gas levels in the pond. In winter, things change when the surface of the pond freezes. The ice prevents the gases from being exchanged between the water and the air. Without gas exchange, the level of CO_2 in water increases, and if the level gets too high, the animals start to die. When fish die in winter, it is usually the high CO_2 levels that kill them, not the cold temperatures.

Anything that causes the top layer of water to move will increase the speed at which gases exchange. Wind making ripples on the water increases air exchange that helps to maintain a balanced ecosystem. Moving water with pumps, waterfalls, and fountains have the same effect as wind, but they are not needed in a properly made natural pond.

There is one final process taking place in your pond that can have a dramatic effect on the oxygen levels in water, and that is decomposition. Both animals and plants produce waste products. All types of animals, including bacteria, poop in the water, and plants shed leaves, seeds, and flowers into the water. When plants and animals die, they add even more organic matter to the pond. All of this organic matter eventually decomposes. This decomposition process uses oxygen, and produces CO_2.

It is critical that a pond maintain correct oxygen and carbon dioxide levels. The best way to ensure that this happens is to take a balanced approach. Keep the number of organisms in a balance to each other. Too many fish requires more oxygen. Too much algae produces too much CO_2. Not enough surface area relative to the total volume of water means that the air exchange at the surface of the water will not be adequate.

Moderation is the key. These topics will be revisited as we go through the design process. Proper design of the pond will eliminate the need for pumps and ensure that you don't have to worry about oxygen levels.

Nutrients

The term "nutrient" can be defined as a substance, either element or compound, that promotes growth and health in living things. The main nutrients we are interested in are the nutrients that plants use. They are the same compounds found in fertilizer—the nitrogen, phosphorus, potassium, and other minor elements.

Nutrients are critical to plants. They absorb the nutrients either through their roots, or in plants like algae that don't have roots, through their cell walls. In both cases, the nutrients are necessary for the plant to grow and carry out key functions like photosynthesis.

Plants use 20 to 30 different nutrients, but most of these are required in very small amounts that are usually found in pond water. The nutrients needed the most include nitrogen, phosphorus, and potassium. Potassium is rarely deficient in established ponds, and we can ignore it. Nitrogen and phosphorus are two nutrients that pond owners need to understand better.

The common form of phosphorus is a molecule called phosphate (PO_4), which at low levels is good for the growth of plants and bacteria. The problem with phosphate is that it accumulates in ponds and can cause problems.

The water you used to fill the pond will contain some phosphate. Water running off nearby fields will carry phosphate into the pond, adding significant amounts if the field was recently fertilized. The rocks used to line the edge of the pond will probably contain phosphorus that will slowly leach into the water. The food used to feed fish will add more phosphorus. Insects and animals that enter the pond will add phosphate when they die, as does plant material when it decomposes in the pond.

Phosphate is a salt that remains behind in the pond after water evaporates. This is the same process you see when boiling water evaporates and leaves the salt deposit behind inside your kettle. As water evaporates over time, the phosphate levels in the pond will increase.

A very similar process has been going on in nature. Over the past 40 years, most lawn fertilizer contained high levels of phosphate, much more than the plants need. The excess washed into local rivers and lakes where it started to accumulate. Soaps that contained high phosphate levels added to the accumulation. All of this excess phosphate in our waterways led to algae blooms, among other problems. Algae grow best with high levels of phosphate.

The phosphate in most lawn fertilizer has now been removed since most soil in North America has plenty of phosphorus and does not need more. Soap products have also been modified to contain far less phosphate. In the last 10 to 20 years, we have seen a steady improvement in algae levels of local waterways.

It is important to design and maintain your pond to minimize the accumulation of phosphate.

Nitrogen, a major nutrient for plants and the one that may be in short supply, is available in several chemical forms. The air we breathe is 80 percent nitrogen, but it is in the form of a gas, N_2. Plants and animals cannot use this nitrogen, but some types of bacteria can. Nitrogen is also found in nitrate and ammonium, which plants and microbes can use.

Microbes, particularly bacteria, convert one form of nitrogen to another as shown in figure 2. They are able to take nitrogen gas from the air and turn it into the other forms of nitrogen. This is critical for plant growth. They also take nitrate and ammonium and convert them back to a nitrogen gas, which escapes from the water into the air. This last point is very important. Unlike phosphate, the microbes are able to remove excess nitrogen from pond water.

Another form of nitrogen found in water is ammonia, which for the purposes of our discussion is the same as ammonium. Ammonium is a

Nitrogen Cycle

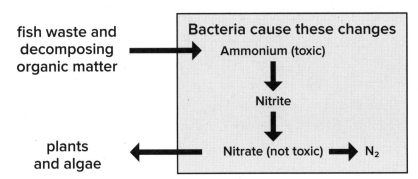

FIGURE 2
Nitrogen cycle

waste product of animals and is produced during the decomposition of organic matter. Unfortunately, this form of nitrogen is deadly to animals even at low levels. Fortunately, bacteria convert ammonium to nitrate, which is then safe for animals.

Since ammonium is so toxic to animals, the levels must be kept low. Keeping fish levels low reduces fish waste that in turn reduces ammonium levels. Excluding fertilizer will also maintain lower levels. As I explain later, the main way to control ammonium levels is through the use of microbes.

Two other nutrients are calcium and magnesium, and most pond water will have enough of them for plant growth. Rocks in the water will add more of both. These are the salts that make tap water hard. If your tap water is hard, you are adding more calcium and magnesium each time you add some to your pond and their levels can get too high. This is one good reason to use rainwater to top up your pond.

Like phosphate, these two salts will accumulate over time because they have no way to escape into the air. As water evaporates, it will leave the salts behind to slowly accumulate. These two nutrients are not harmful to animals except in very high concentrations, but eventually they may pose a problem in a pond.

pH

The pH of your water indicates how acidic or alkaline it is. A pH value of 7 is neutral—neither acidic nor alkaline. A value above 7 indicates the water is alkaline, and below 7 it is acidic. All aquatic life-forms have an optimum range in which they want to live. Most life-forms can live outside this range, but then they are more likely to have diseases and nutrient deficiencies.

Plants like to be in a range of 6 to 7.5. Fish prefer a pH between 7 and 8 and will die below 5 and above 9. Plants are a bit more flexible, but you might have to select them carefully at extreme pH ranges.

The original pH of the pond will be determined by the pH of the water used to fill it. Over time biological processes will add CO_2 to the water making it more acidic. The pH also varies depending on the time of day. During the day, plants under the water, including algae, are using up the CO_2 for photosynthesis and the pH goes up. At night, photosynthesis stops and plants produce CO_2 that lowers the pH. The pH is lowest before sunup and highest at dusk. This daily swing depends on a number of factors, but can easily change by a full pH unit.

Rain has a natural pH of 5.5 and can be more acidic in high pollution areas. A heavy rain can reduce the pH of the pond significantly.

The pH also affects the toxicity of ammonium, which is more toxic at high pH, and less so at low pH.

By now you might be feeling that all of this chemistry is very confusing and that pond keeping might not be for you. Don't worry about that. One of the benefits of making a natural pond over the traditional designs is that you don't have to be concerned about pH and ammonium levels. I'll show you how to design the pond so that nature does all of this for you.

Algae

Most algae are green, but brown ones do exist. Although they don't have roots or leaves in the traditional sense, most are able to photosynthesize. There are many types of algae but we can simplify things by considering only two types; filamentous or string algae and planktonic algae.

Planktonic algae consist of single cells that are fully self-sufficient. They are able to reproduce, absorb CO_2 and nutrients, and make food using photosynthesis. The individual cells are too small to see by eye. In a pond, they make the water look green, blue-green, or brown, and if there are a lot of them, the water looks like pea soup. This coloration is called an algae bloom and can involve many different species of algae.

Filamentous algae are also green single-cell organisms, but they join together to form long hair-like strands—the filaments. The algae attach themselves to rocks under water, and as more algae cells are added, the strands get longer and longer, forming large floating masses of stringy clumps. When it floats on the surface of the water it is called pond scum. This is the algae most people want to get rid of. Filamentous algae also photosynthesize.

All ponds have some algae, and this is actually good for the ecosystem because they serve as a food source for protozoans, insects, and fish. They are a vital part of the aquatic food chain, but too much algae becomes a nuisance. It is not aesthetically pleasing, and it can interfere with fishing and swimming. Excess algae can have a detrimental effect on the balanced ecosystem. During the night, algae produces CO_2, and too much algae can increase the level to a point where it becomes toxic to animals. The excess CO_2 also lowers the pH, which can also cause problems.

An algae bloom grows quickly filling the pond, and then it crashes, as it outgrows the availability of nutrients and cells start to die. This seems like a good thing, but the dead algae falls to the bottom of the pond, starts to decompose, and can produce high levels of CO_2 and ammonium, both of which are problems for the animal population.

It all comes down to having a balanced ecosystem. Some algae is acceptable and good for the pond. Too much is a problem.

Animals

Birds and mammals are not affected too much by the biology and chemistry going on in the pond. They use the water mostly for drinking, and if it is not suitable for them, they will just go somewhere else. They do, however, depend on the pond for food, and so it is essential that amphibians, fish, and insects are prospering in the pond so that they attract mammals and birds—provided that is what you want.

Amphibians are a central part of pond life, and their natural habitats have been decimated in recent years. Building backyard ponds is one way to help them survive, while at the same time providing enjoyment for us. Amphibians are very sensitive to chemicals in the water and to sudden changes in water quality. If frogs live and breed in your pond, it is a reliable indicator that your water quality is good.

Very little is known about the water quality required by insects, but you will find them in just about every pond. Although the type may vary from pond to pond, there are always lots of insects in the water. If your water source is drinking water, it will be of a suitable quality for insects.

Fish are sensitive to poor water quality, which will make them more susceptible to diseases and possible death. It is difficult to treat fish in a pond for sickness, so it is better to prevent it by keeping the water quality high.

One of the main requirements for fish is the oxygen level. When it gets too low, fish can't breathe, they get sick and die. The fish will tell you when the levels are getting low by spending most of their time near the surface where oxygen levels are higher. If they continually gulp for air, they are telling you that oxygen levels have reached a critical point.

Because of their large size, relative to other pond life, fish also produce a lot of waste, which contains ammonium and other organic material. The ammonium can cause problems right away if levels are too high. The other organic material is slowly decomposed by microbes into nutrients, which in high levels cause long-term problems. The easiest way to control the amount of fish waste is to reduce the number of fish.

Fish are the one pond animal that people want to feed. All other animals find their own food, but for some reason, people feel that fish need to be fed. That may be true in an aquarium, but it is not necessary in a natural pond. Let the fish feed themselves. They will eat algae, which reduces the algae problem, and insects and their larvae, keeping their population in check. If there is not enough food available, fish will simply grow slower, which means less fish waste. I never feed the goldfish in my pond, and they grow and breed all on their own. Stop interfering with nature and let your fish be part of the balanced ecosystem.

Trees and Shrubs

Although trees and shrubs don't affect the pond directly, they do significantly influence the pond's ecosystem. Trees can provide a significant amount of shade that will reduce the amount of algae in the pond, since algae only grows well in full sun. The reduced light under trees also affects other plants. Most pond plants like to have full sun or at least partial sun. A pond with too many trees will not be able to grow enough healthy plants. Adding shrubs around the edge of a pond not only looks more natural than a field or grass, but it also provides shelter for larger animals and birds. It makes it easier for them to visit the pond for a drink. The shrubs also attract more insects to the pond ecosystem, which in turn attracts more birds and predatory insects like dragonflies. The life around the outside of the pond extends the size of the pond ecosystem, and can easily include your entire backyard.

Trees and shrubs sound like they are a perfect addition to a pond, but they also cause a problem. In fall, these woody plants shed their leaves which drop into the water. Even evergreen plants loose leaves and needles at some point in their development. All of this extra organic matter will decompose and increase the nutrient levels that make it easier for algae to grow.

Plants

This book is all about creating natural ponds, and in a natural design, plants play a critical role. You might think that this role is an aesthetic one since all of the plants growing in and around a pond make it look natural. Although true, that is not the main reason to add plants. They are critical for maintaining water quality and keeping algae in check.

The following discussion applies to all plants that have their roots in the water, including cattails growing along the shoreline, water lilies on the water, or even fully submerged plants. They all need CO_2, water, and nutrients to photosynthesize. Plants that have leaves above the surface get CO_2 from the air; those that only have leaves below the surface extract CO_2 from the water.

Since water is readily available, there is one key requirement, nutrients, that most plants absorb through their roots. Submerged plants also absorb them through their leaves or cell walls. Nutrients are used in photosynthesis and all other functions in a plant, including growth. Throughout this chapter, we have discussed ways in which nutrients enter the pond. Plants are the only natural way to remove nutrients from the water, keeping the water quality high for other pond inhabitants.

Algae compete with other plants for nutrients. Fortunately, they only thrive if the nutrient level is high. Other plants will prosper in water with lower amounts of nutrients, but algae will not. This is the secret to maintaining a natural algae-free pond. It has to be designed so that there is a good balance between the number of plants and the amount of nutrients being added to the pond. As long as plants can keep the nutrient level low, algae will not grow.

Plants can do more than just keep nutrient levels low. Floating plants like water lilies cover the surface, which shades the water. As light levels are reduced, the amount of algae is also lowered since they only grow in high light levels. Floating plants do double duty in the pond; they reduce nutrient levels and available light.

Microbes

The term "microbe" is a general label for a wide variety of small microscopic life-forms, including bacteria, fungi, and single-celled and multi-celled animals. It normally includes planktonic algae, but I will exclude algae when I refer to microbes.

You can't see individual microbes with your naked eye, but pond water has thousands of different species. You can see them when they congregate in vast numbers on the pond liner or on rocks. Many people feel that these communities, frequently called slime, should be removed; most pond books and websites recommend a yearly cleaning. They suggest going to such an extreme as emptying the pond and scrubbing the liner.

These microbe communities play a critical role in the ecosystem of the pond. In maintaining a natural pond, you try to grow the microbes and keep them healthy and happy—you don't scrub them away.

High levels of ammonium, which is produced by fish and decomposing organic matter, can kill pond animals. The microbes, especially the bacteria, are able to digest the ammonium and convert it to nitrates which are much less toxic to animals. In a normal pond, filtration systems are used to house these microbes. The natural pond just uses slime on the pond liner and rocks to accomplish the same thing.

Microbes also use nutrients to grow. As nutrient levels get high, microbes multiply into large communities and use up excess nutrients, competing with the algae and plants. Unfortunately, too much growth causes nutrient levels to become scarce and microbes start to die. These dead microbes add to the problem of too much organic matter, which leads to more nutrients and the cycle starts all over again. A healthy plant community helps keep these growth cycles in check.

One of the most important groups of microbes is bacteria. Of the two basic types, aerobic bacteria like to live in an oxygen-rich environment just like humans. The word "aerobic" means "requiring oxygen." The other type, anaerobic, do not require as much oxygen. They live and prosper in water that has a very low level of oxygen.

A healthy pond contains mostly aerobic bacteria. These are the ones you want because they play a big role in keeping the water clear and balanced. Most ponds also have some anaerobic bacteria, found on the bottom where oxygen levels are low due to decomposing organic matter.

The bottom of the pond accumulates most of the organic matter as it falls into the water. Tree leaves, dead animals, and dead microbes all settle there, creating what is known as pond sludge. As this organic matter decomposes, it uses up the oxygen at the bottom and makes a perfect breeding ground for anaerobic bacteria, which continue the decomposition process but more slowly than aerobic bacteria. With time the sludge layer usually gets thicker and thicker.

The sludge itself does not cause a great problem, but the anaerobic bacteria produce hydrogen sulfide, also called rotten egg gas, which is poisonous to pond life. This heavy gas tends to stay at the bottom of the pond. As long as it is not disturbed, you will not notice it. If it is disturbed, you will definitely smell the problem.

Maintaining Balance in the Ecosystem

People talk about balanced ecosystems as if nature were able to maintain them indefinitely. To some extent this is true. If you compare a native pond this year to last year, you will probably not see much difference. Even over ten years, things don't change a lot, and it is not surprising that the system is considered to be "in balance." But it's not.

Every native pond is evolving and changing over time. It is disappearing. The pond slowly fills with organic material and more and more plants, eventually becoming a bog as the water level lowers. In the distant future, it will dry up completely.

The pond you build will also want to go through the same changes. If left completely alone, it will eventually be dry land. The good news is that it takes very little effort to stop this natural progression. Your pond can be kept balanced and unchanged for a long time.

This chapter has discussed a number of biological and chemical systems that happen in every pond. I am sure that you have noticed that they are all interrelated. Each system needs to be managed and controlled, or else it affects all other systems. You might be sitting there scratching your head, thinking that you can't possibly control all of these systems correctly. You are right—you can't.

The natural pond system described in this book is designed so that it takes care of all of these systems for you, automatically. All you have to do is design the pond correctly from the start and follow a few simple rules.

Don't have too many fish because they poop too much. Use lots of plants because they keep nutrient levels low so algae do not grow. Include water lilies to shade the water. Don't clean your pond because the microbes are working for you.

The remaining chapters will address the design requirements and the pond rules in more detail. You will start to understand how easy it really is to have a natural pond with a balanced ecosystem.

Display pond at a nursery.

Above: Natural swimming pool designed by Organic Pools.
Left: New pond ready for planting.
Below: Siberian iris.

Above: Tropical waterlily.
Left: Large pond used for swimming and raising trout.
Below: Lined pond.

Above: A dock provides easy access to the pond.
Left: Finished pond.
Below: Hardy waterlily.

Above: Marsh marigold.
Left: Tropical waterlily.
Below: Author's hilltop pond and oriental teahouse.

Above: Pickerel weed.
Left top: Pond built into a small hill.
Left middle: Formal pond.
Left bottom: Pond built using native stones.
Below: Umbrella palm.
Opposite: A bridge provides good viewing points for wildlife.

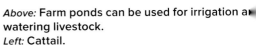

Above: Farm ponds can be used for irrigation and watering livestock.
Left: Cattail.
Below: Japanese Iris.

CHAPTER 2

Environmental Benefits

The day after filling my first pond with water, frogs had already moved in. The vegetation was not yet planted, and I am sure there was nothing for them to eat, but they were there ready to enjoy a new life. Creating a pond adds a new ecosystem that will attract all kinds of life that you normally do not see in a garden. It is a wonderful way to bring nature to your yard.

Pond Ecosystem

All kinds of animals and insects will find your new pond. Some of this life is microscopic. Bacteria, fungi, and algae quickly float in on the air currents. The water gives these organisms a place to live and grow. Once they are present, larger animals such as rotifers and Hydra will move in and eat the bacteria, fungi, and algae. These animals are very small; you won't notice them unless without your magnifying glass. Rotifers and Hydra are eaten in turn by larger animals like arthropods. All of these small animals are vital to the development of your pond.

Some insects, like mosquitoes and dragonflies, lay their eggs in the water, and after hatching, they eat the smaller pond life. Frogs and toads also lay their eggs in the water, and the tadpoles consume the small animals and insect larvae. If you put fish in the pond, they will enjoy a meal of small tadpoles and mosquito larvae.

As the tadpoles mature, they attract even larger animals like snakes and some birds. Maybe a mink will come by for a snack, and you are almost certainly going to see some herons if they live in your neck of the woods.

You probably knew that all of these animals feed on each other. What is surprising is that they all find your pond and start living in it or beside it with no effort on your part. All you need to do is to provide a hole in the ground and some water. Then wait for the magic to happen.

Plants also play a big role in this pond ecosystem. In the following chapters, I'll suggest that you add plants to the pond, but even this may not be necessary. Two different species of cattails arrived in my pond without being planted. One arrived the first summer, and it does not grow naturally near my home. Other native plants have also settled in on their own.

Plants provide food for certain microbes and animals and shelter from predators. The dragonfly nymph will climb up cattail stems to emerge as a flying insect. Frogs love to sit on lily pads and catch flying insects.

Breeding Site for Amphibians

Frogs, toads, and salamanders are common in many locations. Like most amphibians, they need to lay their eggs in water. Once the eggs hatch, the tadpoles live in water until they become adults. Some amphibians spend most of their life on land; others spend much of it in water. Water is vital to their survival.

Many amphibians are threatened in the wild because their natural wetlands and ponds are disappearing. They are also very sensitive to chemical pollutants and are easily killed. Building a pond will help them survive.

I have a natural pond close to my property, and the last two winters were exceptionally cold. The native amphibians can handle cold, but they can't handle winter thaws that are followed by very cold temperatures, which is exactly what has happened the last two years. As a result, I have seen a dramatic decline in frog populations. I used to be able to count over 30 sitting around the pond, and now I am lucky to find 12. They breed in my pond, and I know it is helping them to increase their local populations.

Why should you care? Amphibians are very beneficial to your garden. They eat all kinds of insects and slugs. The frogs and toads are part of my garden's natural pest control system. Besides, they sing for me in the spring and provide entertainment all summer long. All I have to do is provide the water.

Dragonflies and Mosquitoes

Mosquitoes lay their eggs in shallow water that is not moving too much. The hatching larvae will live in the water until they emerge as adult insects. Mosquitoes are a potential problem. They not only bite, but they can carry diseases. Everyone is advised not to allow any standing water because mosquitoes will breed in it. How can a pond, without moving water, be a good idea?

Mosquito larvae are a delicacy for many animals living in the pond. Fish love them. If you have any concern about breeding mosquitoes, add a few goldfish, and they will take care of them. Frogs also eat mosquito larvae, and if some live in your pond, you really don't need the fish.

Ponds also attract dragonflies that lay their eggs in the water. As the eggs hatch, they produce a very large nymph that is an expert hunter. One of their favorite foods is the mosquito larvae. The nymph will grow and hatch into the adult dragonfly that hunts insects, including the adult mosquito. Once I see dragonflies, I know that the mosquito season is almost at an end.

The mosquito is a food source for many life-forms, including amphibians, insects, and even small birds. Contrary to popular belief, most bats don't eat many mosquitoes—they are just too small to be worth the effort. Some very tiny bats do eat mosquitoes.

Birds and Mammals

Your pond will also attract birds and large animals that will come for a drink. A shallow beach area allows small animals like birds to get close to the water and makes it easier for rodents and other small mammals to get a drink. I routinely have skunks, raccoons, possums, wild turkeys, heron, mink, fox, coyotes, and deer visit the pond—but not usually at the same time.

Not all of these visitors are entirely welcome since some will eat fish and frogs, but they all play a critical part of the pond ecosystem. The fox eats the skunks, racoons, and wild turkeys. The coyotes eat deer. I don't have a lot of rodent problems in the garden because I keep the local coyotes and foxes well hydrated with my pond.

Birds are a very good defense against insect pests in the garden. The pond provides them with water, and it attracts insects that in turn attract the birds.

The pond design presented in this book will encourage such visitors and make it easy for them to get out of the pond should they fall in. It also limits the damage done to pond liners by animals like minks and makes it difficult for herons to catch fish.

Water Conservation

With water becoming a precious commodity, many communities implement water bans. The pond that is built for pleasure can act as an emergency water source. During a ban, you can use the water to keep your gardens growing well. On larger properties, a pond can be used as a regular water source for your garden. These large ponds are more fully described in chapter 9.

In an area that has regular water bans, it is likely that you don't get enough rain in summer to keep your pond full. There are steps you can take to improve this situation. House gutters can direct rain into your pond, which then acts like a very large rain barrel, collecting water to be used during a drought. For more information on this, see the section on rain gardens.

The location of your pond can significantly affect the amount of water it collects. A slope on your property can be used to direct runoff straight into the pond. In such a location, even a small amount of rain can fill the pond, and it is a good way to reduce the amount of water running into the street and city storm water systems.

Environmental Awareness

A natural pond is an ideal tool for teaching yourself and your children about nature. Instead of just reading about it, you can observe it in real time. You will find all kinds of interesting things happen in the pond. By watching, listening, and enjoying the pond, your whole family will learn about the wonders of the natural world. Seeing a tadpole grow into a frog can positively impact children for a lifetime. They might even become the world's next great naturalist.

Less Lawn

According to the Environmental Protection Agency, the United States has 40 million acres of lawn, which uses 7 billion gallons of water daily and 3 million tons of fertilizer. Mowing them takes 800 million gallons of gasoline—the oil spilled by the *Exxon Valdez* was only 11 million gallons, and it was considered an environmental catastrophe. Lawns are a major environmental problem.

Gas-powered lawn mowers also emit high levels of carbon monoxide, volatile organic compounds, and nitrogen oxides. Adding a pond to your garden reduces the amount of lawn, which in turn reduces the use of gasoline and fertilizer. Ponds are good for the environment, especially if you remove the lawn around the pond and turn that into a garden as well.

Permaculture Food Sources

Permaculture is both a philosophy of life and a method of gardening that focuses on reducing our effect on the environment. Natural ponds fit with this philosophy. Many pond plants can be food sources. Arrowhead (wapato), wild rice, lotus, and water lilies will provide food for people and livestock. Larger ponds can be used to raise fish and waterfowl.

Cattails can be used in many ways. The roots, shoots, stems, and pollen are all edible. New spring shoots can be peeled and eaten raw as a delicacy. The roots can be made into sweet syrup to pour over pancakes made from cattail root flour. As a poultice, the pounded roots are reported to help fight infections, heal broken blisters, and soothe insect stings. Cattails are a grocery store and pharmacy all in one plant.

Here is a list of some water plants that are used for food:

- Arrowhead (*Sagittaria latifolia*)—edible tubers
- Lotus (*Nelumbo nucifera*)—edible tubers, young leaves and seeds
- Taro (*Colocasia esculento*)—corms are edible once cooked (poisonous when raw)
- Water chestnut (*Eleocharis dulcis*)—edible corms
- Watercress (*Nasturtium officinale*)—edible leaves
- Water lily (*Nymphaea* spp.)—edible roots
- Water spinach (*Ipomoea aquatica*)—edible leaves
- Wild rice (*Zizania* sp.)—edible seeds

The design for an edible water garden is really no different than the natural design presented in this book. You might want to have larger planting shelves to maximize space for food plants. Give some thought about harvesting the plants. Consider adding several high stones on the planting shelves that will allow you to walk out to your plants and keep your feet dry.

CHAPTER 3

Natural Looking Designs

Lots of people talk about natural ponds, but what are they? How do we define a natural pond? How do you know your pond is or is not natural looking? These seem like simple questions, but they are not easy to answer. In this chapter, I'll try to provide some answers to these questions by discussing the aesthetic side of the design process.

A good way to understand what natural really means is to look at different ponds. If I show you several pictures, you will probably have very little trouble separating those that look natural from those that look man-made. You will also notice some that fit in the gray area between the two extremes. We have a kind of sixth sense that helps us identify naturalness.

You can pick out a natural looking pond from a pile of pictures, but can you explain why it looks natural? For most people, this is not an easy task.

In order to build and design a natural looking pond, you should understand which features make a pond look natural. One of the best ways to gain this knowledge is to study native ponds. Go for a walk and look at a variety of real ponds, large and small, some in open fields as well as ones in wooded areas. As you look at each one, ask these questions. What is it about this pond that makes it look natural? Do some parts look artificial and man-made?

Surf the internet and look at more ponds. This is a great way to see man-made ponds in backyards. Examine each one, ask the same questions you asked about native ponds, and list your answers. This analysis will help you understand what "naturalness" means to you.

One of the biggest mistakes people make in designing gardens is to follow the advice of others, following rules dictated by so called experts. You will be happier with your garden if you design it for yourself. If you like it, it is the right design. The same goes for pond design. We all have different opinions about what makes a pond look natural, and that is ok. You are building the pond for your enjoyment, and you should design it the way you want.

On the following pages, I will critique some ponds and help you learn the process of analyzing ponds. It is then up to you to reach your own conclusions.

Native Ponds

Why would a native pond look unnatural? Doesn't everything made by Mother Earth look natural? Not necessarily. We each have an idea of what is natural, and we don't all agree on these characteristics. Many of our native ponds have been altered by man. The pond in the middle of a field probably had trees around it at some point. The view from beside the pond may now include houses and fences in the distance. In most urban areas, even the natural areas have been altered in some way.

The pictures on the next few pages are all from native ponds. I'll analyze them and try to better understand what makes them look natural or man-made.

Small Native Woodland Pond (Figure 3)
Characteristics that make the pond look natural:
- There are no visible man-made structures.
- The grass at the back grows right into the water.
- Tree debris has not been cleaned up.
- Plant material, including trees, grows right down to the water's edge.

- The background consists of several different varieties of trees and shrubs that don't look very orderly.

FIGURE 3
Small native woodland pond

Characteristics that make the pond look man-made:
- There is really no indication that man has ever been here except that one of the stumps looks as if it has been sawn off.

Large Open Pond (Figure 4)
Characteristics that make the pond look natural:
- The pond scum is found on many ponds in mid to late summer— it is part of the ecosystem.
- Shrubs on the left side come right down to the water and branches overhang the water.
- The land around the pond slopes down to the water, making it look like a natural place for water to collect.

FIGURE 4
Large open pond

Characteristics that make the pond look man-made:
- The grass in the lower left corner and the far side look as if it has been maintained.
- The edge on the far side looks very regular with no logs or rocks.
- There are no large trees close to the pond, which gives the impression that someone has removed them; it looks too neat.

Large Lake (Figure 5)
Characteristics that make the pond look natural:
- The rocks are well-worn with rounded edges showing their age and randomly located.
- Some rocks sit right in the water; the larger ones exposed, the smaller ones submerged.

- The rocks on the far shoreline are clearly visible but mostly covered with vegetation.
- The trees are all similar. In most natural places, you find a few species growing together, unlike gardens that tend to include many different species.
- There is a definite lack of flowers. Those you find in nature tend to be less dramatic than the ones we have in our gardens.

Characteristics that make the pond look man-made:
- None of the trees come down to the water.
- No logs or plant material are in the water.
- Shoreline is quite straight with no irregularities.

FIGURE 5
Author canoeing into a large lake in central Labrador, Canada.

Man-made Ponds

Although ponds look artificial when they include elements that are recognized as man-made, it can be difficult to exclude them in a backyard. Fences are certainly not natural looking, but they serve a clear purpose, as do some man-made lawns.

The materials you select to include in your design can have a large influence on the naturalness of the garden. For example, gravel or concrete can be used to make a pathway. Both are processed material, but we perceive gravel as being much more natural.

How natural a product looks is also influenced by how the material is used. Square concrete paving stones that are laid end to end, in a straight line, look very formal. The same stones in a random pattern, with grass growing between them, make the garden appear less formal, more natural looking.

Although backyard ponds can't be all natural, in the following section, I analyze some man-made ponds and develop guidelines for making them look as natural as possible.

Pond Built into a Small Hill (Figure 6)

Characteristics that make the pond look natural:

- The pond is well situated in the landscape. The ground slopes towards the viewer, and the pond is located at the bottom of it, providing an ideal spot to add the waterfall. Even without the waterfall, the pond is where we expect it, where water naturally collects.
- A small number of floating plants are unevenly distributed.
- The rocks vary in size, shape, and color.

Characteristics that make the pond look man-made:

- The placement of rocks on the far shore is too regular and looks like a man-made stone wall. Behind the shoreline is another row, with each rock butting up to the one beside it. Behind that is another row of rocks.

FIGURE 6
Pond built into
a small hill.

- The plantings on the near shore consist of unnatural looking clumps planted in a straight line around the perimeter.
- Some of the plants are not normally seen beside water, at least not in North America. In the wild, hostas grow beside water, but most people don't think of them as waterside plants, so they look out of place.
- There is no vegetation hanging down over the far bank to hide part of the rock wall.
- All of the vegetation on the far shore consists of small plants— it really needs variation and more height. Imagine how different it would look with a single weeping Japanese maple hanging its branches into the water.
- The pond has an oval shape that is made more prominent by the plantings around it following this shape.
- Two flagstones, at the bottom center of the picture, look artificial, but they do serve a purpose by providing access to the water. Sometimes a compromise is necessary between aesthetics and functionality.

Pond Built using Native Stones (Figure 7)

Characteristics that make the pond look natural:

- The rocks used in this pond are very natural looking, with rounded edges and indentations worn by the passage of time. They even have lichen growing on them. In fact they were collected from the fields surrounding the property—you can't get more natural than that.
- The iris in the lower left corner is a good choice since they are naturally found along pond edges.

Characteristics that make the pond look man-made:

- This is a good-looking pond, but it demonstrates the single worst thing you can do in a natural pond: show the liner. If that is visible, the pond will never look natural.
- The way in which the rocks have been stacked looks artificial—clearly not a natural placement.
- The vegetation does not hide enough of the rocks around the perimeter. Compare this rock edge with the one in figure 5.

FIGURE 7
Pond built using native stones from the property.

- What about the ornaments, the heron and the water-spitting frog? Do they fit in a natural pond? Clearly they are not natural, but if we accept the position that a backyard pond will never be 100 percent natural, then these ornaments can have a place. They add a bit of whimsy and interest to the garden so long as they are not overdone. I would keep the heron and get rid of the frog. You should feel free to add whatever makes you happy.
- Grasses, which look natural in a pond area, have been added on the far shore, but in this case, there are three types of grasses, one clump each. Several clumps of one type would look better.

Formal Pond (Figure 8)

Characteristics that make the pond look natural:

- Nothing! I have included this picture to make a point. Ponds can look great without being natural. If you like this style of pond, build it. You can still use most of the information in this book to help you create a low-maintenance formal pond.

FIGURE 8
Formal pond.

Characteristics that make the pond look man-made:

- The shape of the pond is symmetrical, giving it a very formal look.
- The edging stone has been cut into regular shapes and seems unnaturally flat.
- A lawn edges the stones; manicured lawns never look natural.
- Planting is done in pots that are visible above the waterline. There is nothing wrong with using pots, but they should be hidden.

Dislplay Pond (Figure 9)

Characteristics that make the pond look natural:

- The irregular round rocks show the age of time and vary in size. They don't look like stacked rocks.
- Plants are growing over the rocks and will eventually grow right into the water. The far side will look quite natural in another year or two.

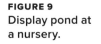

FIGURE 9
Display pond at
a nursery.

- Rocks have been placed in the bottom, which is very natural. I don't recommend doing this since it becomes very hard to clean the pond if needed. In deeper ponds, the stones are not needed, but in shallow ones like this, they do enhance the aesthetics.
- There are two large rocks behind the fake bird. Most people would not place them this far back from the edge; this is precisely what makes them look natural.

Characteristics that make the pond look man-made:
- The liner is well hidden, but it does show around the rocks on the near side.
- The oval shape is very traditional. It is difficult to make a small pond like this look natural. More plants in the pond would help hide the shape.
- The pot in the lower left corner is clearly man-made. It has a traditional spiky plant in the center and lower reddish leaves around the outside.
- The planting is far too variable for such a small pond—it looks like a typical garden instead of a native spot.

Author's Pond (Figure 10)
Characteristics that make the pond look natural:
- Rocks along the edge are well hidden by plants.
- Some rocks are located right in the water, which is rarely seen in man-made ponds, but is common in nature.
- The cattails are a native plant and seem to belong.
- The background trees and shrubs are natural looking and don't have an overly manicured look.

Characteristics that make the pond look man-made:
- The building and deck are clearly man-made, but they help visitors enjoy the pond.
- The water lily is pink, which is not a color native to this location.

FIGURE 10
Author's hilltop pond
and oriental teahouse.

• The shrubs on the near shore are also not native and look a bit unnatural. As a plantaholic, I love collecting different plants. I have to balance a desire for natural with my personal obsession, and that is ok.

How Natural Can You Get?

Now that you are familiar with some characteristics that make ponds look natural, it is time to think about your own design. Which of these characteristics will you incorporate into your pond? How natural will it look? It is best to give some thought to this before you start digging the hole. Make a list and edit it as you work through the design process.

In reality, it is difficult to be 100 percent natural on a normal-sized lot. You will see your house, and probably neighboring houses, and may have fences and sheds to deal with. In your design process, you will need to make compromises between what is practicable and what is natural. You also have to satisfy your personal desires—you might really like that water-spitting frog. In the end, the only thing that matters is that you enjoy your pond.

The Borrowed View

The term "borrowed view" was introduced by designers of Japanese gardens. They placed a high value on the view they got of their neighbor's yard. Do the neighbors have trees or shrubs that could be "borrowed" as a backdrop for your pond? Locating the pond to take advantage of this vegetation might give it a much more natural look. If you don't have a great borrowed view, do you have trees or shrubs that can be used as a backdrop? If not, consider adding shrubs behind the pond to provide a natural looking backdrop and probably hide a fence. If you do add shrubs make sure they will look natural. Stay away from formal clipped hedges that seem so popular at the back of a yard. Have variation in height, shape, and leaf coloring. Many native shrubs will fit the bill.

Enjoy the Pond

The last picture we analyzed had a building and deck beside the pond. That is my pond, which from the start was designed to be very natural looking. So why did I include the building and deck? The Japanese teahouse was added to meet the design requirements of the large garden that needed a focal point to draw people up to the hilltop, where it sits facing the main garden. The picture shows the side and back of the building that faces the other way. I had to compromise between the design needs of the semi-formal main garden and those of a natural pond. You will probably have to make similar compromises in your backyard.

You will want to enjoy your pond, and part of that enjoyment requires easy access to the water. There is no point having fish and frogs if you can't see them. You can provide access to the water with some flat stone work, a sandy beach, or even a deck. In my case, the back of the building is very rustic and reminiscent of a poor man's cabin. The deck was a good choice since it fit this theme—every cabin should have a deck down by the lake. Being a foot or more higher than the water's edge, the deck also provides a better view into the pond and over the surface reflections.

In a flat backyard, the deck may look out of place. You could consider a bridge over the pond, and I'll show you how to build the footings in chapter 5. You could also create a stone or gravel patio next to the pond. Think about how you will use the pond and what is needed around it to facilitate your enjoyment of it. Also think about access for maintenance, such as accessing the edge to maintain the plants.

Stones, Stones, and More Stones

Stones are an essential part of any pond and can look natural or man-made. Square concrete patio blocks look more man-made than flagstones. Flagstones look more man-made than gravel, especially if the edge of the gravel area is irregular and obscured by plants.

It is best for both aesthetic and financial reasons to use local materials. Stones that look natural in Florida won't look natural in Ontario, and shipping is very expensive and wastes valuable natural resources. Local is always better.

Ponds look best when the stones vary in shapes and sizes, like what you find in nature. Really large ones look great, but they can be difficult to move without heavy equipment. Medium stones can be rolled into place using pry bars.

Quarried stone, like armor stone, is very popular for landscape projects, but the sharp edges make them look man-made. Try to find stones with rounded edges or odd shapes. It takes nature millions of years to make these stones, and for that reason, they look natural.

Plants Are Key

The naturalness of a pond is greatly affected by the plants you select, but you will have to balance the desire to have a natural pond with your gardening interests. I am a plantaholic and love growing many different kinds. I'll forgo the best garden design and select one that permits a larger variety of plants. There is nothing wrong with this choice—my garden is there to please me. Your garden needs to please you.

When I analyzed the picture of my pond (figure 10), I mentioned the pink water lily and said it didn't look very natural. The native ponds where I live only have white water lilies. Pink ones look out of place. In your area, pink ones may be common, or maybe there are no water lilies at all. What looks natural in one part of the country may not look natural elsewhere.

This last point applies to all of your selections. Native plants are certainly one option; adding some non-native plants is also ok. If they are selected with care, they will look just as natural as native plants.

We associate grasses with ponds. They like the extra sun an open pond provides, and they usually grow well in such an exposed location. Grasses are mostly tall spiky plants, like iris and cattails (bulrushes). Any plant with a similar shape will also look natural beside the pond. A round, clipped boxwood looks out of place.

Low-growing plantings outside the pond help hide its stone edge. The grasses, irises, and cattails grow upwards and are therefore not suitable. Instead choose plants that stay close to the ground so that they can grow over the rocks and into the water. Low-growing junipers work well, and they can be clipped and trained to maintain the desired shape and size. Weeping Japanese maples add height to the planting and grow down to cover the stones. Unfortunately they grow very slowly, and rabbits like to nibble on them in winter.

Many gardening books recommend bog plants (i.e., marginals) around the perimeter of the pond. They like growing in wet soil, and it seems logical to plant them around a pond, which is where they grow in nature. The problem with a man-made pond is that the soil around the edge can be quite dry. Any rain hitting the liner will flow into the pond, not onto the soil. So the soil under the liner tends to remain dry. Bog plants only grow well in the pond, not around it.

The type of plants around the pond can have a dramatic effect on the personality of the pond. Low plants will create an open, sunny, exposed feeling. Tall ones will close things in and create a much more intimate experience. Which design would you enjoy more?

Your Final Design

The above information should give you a good starting list of preferences for the aesthetic aspects of design. The next chapter will help you decide on the functional aspects of your project. Refer to this chapter before making your final design decisions, which must be a compromise between aesthetics and function.

CHAPTER 4

Planning and Design

This chapter will help you go through a decision making process to create a plan for your project. While working through the sections, remember that many of them are interrelated, for example, the size of the pond and its location. When going through the process, you will probably have to change your original decisions to meet new requirements. Stay flexible and keep modifying your design as you progress.

It is advisable to write your plan down early in the process. Use lots of paper, and be prepared to discard a lot of it as the plan matures. Include drawings as well as lists of your decisions made or to be made. It is surprising how good an idea sounds while it is in your head. Once on paper, it's not always as good. The act of drawing and writing forces you to more clearly analyze the plan. This also applies to designing the garden and the home.

The pictures in this chapter follow the construction of a new pond from start to finish.

Location

The rest of this chapter will be mostly about practicable considerations for locating the pond. First I want you to think about the aesthetics of design. Where will the pond look its best? What kind of experience do you want from the pond? How do you want to enjoy it? A good way to start is to visualize the pond from inside the house. When you sit or stand inside, what do you see? Would you like that view to include a pond?

When building my waterfall, I positioned it so it was visible from the kitchen table. From this vantage point, I can look out at the waterfall, through a large bay window, every morning for breakfast. A big surprise for me was that I also enjoyed the view in winter when the water fall is covered in snow and ice. It is now a year-round feature for the house.

Do you have patio or plan to add one? It is great to situate the pond next to the patio so that you can get as much enjoyment out of it as possible.

A pond can also be put near the back of the property. Make it a destination at the end of a walk through your garden. Plan to put a bench there so you will sit and enjoy it while sipping morning coffee.

Ideally, you will be able to view your pond from several locations in the garden, but there will always be one that is most important. It might be the patio or it might be the bench you sit on while enjoying the pond. Stand at this spot and look beyond the imaginary pond. What do you see? Is the view pleasing? If the view is not that great, can you relocate the pond to give you a better view? If you don't want to move the pond, consider relocating the primary viewing point. This may require changes to the garden, or it might be as simple as moving a bench. Looking at the same pond from a different direction may greatly enhance the pond experience.

My waterfall is placed so that I see it from both the house and patio. A separate pond, shown in figure 10, is located quite far from the house, at the top of a hill, a destination that takes me through much of the garden. There, facing away from the house, I am fully immersed in wilderness, seeing only trees and shrubs, away from the daily grind of life. Both water features were specifically located to provide these very different experiences. As part of the planning process, you need to decide on the type of experience you want to create.

Legal Issues

Before you start dreaming of your new pond, check with local governments and organizations to understand the regulations for building ponds in your area. Each jurisdiction is different, and all this book can do is suggest places for you to check.

Safety issues are usually controlled at the local level. In my neighborhood, a pool has to be fenced to prevent children from accidently falling into it. A pond does not have the same requirements, which seems odd to me. What is the difference between a pool and a pond? It comes down to intent. If you build something that is intended for swimming, even if it is a pond, then the City considers it to be a pool and requires it to have a fence. If the design is clearly not meant for swimming, even if you could swim in it, it is a pond and requires no fence. This is my situation. Yours will probably be different, so check your own local requirements.

Properties that are located near natural water systems, such as lakes, rivers, and wetlands, are usually controlled by government regulations. You probably can't divert a river to provide water to your pond. In wetlands, you will likely have additional restrictions about what you can and cannot do to change water levels. You might even need a permit to build a pond or have it inspected. The regulations may depend on the size and design of your pond. A detailed list of government regulatory bodies is given in the chapter on large-scale ponds.

Access to Electrical Power

This book recommends a natural pond design that does not require electricity, but you may want to have a source close by, for a variety of reasons. Small ponds can be dug by hand, and you don't need any electrical equipment to do so. Large ones are usually dug by machinery using gasoline or diesel, not electricity. If your design includes wooden structures around the pond, you might want access to electricity for your power tools.

Adding electric lights to a pond can extend the amount of time you can enjoy it. New solar-powered lights are now also a viable option, provided that you are looking for lower light levels.

How will you turn the lights on and off? Will you use a timer at the pond? Do you want to be able to control them from inside the house? Running lights on a timer is an easy system to install, but wastes electricity when you are away or busy doing other things and can't enjoy the outside lights.

When designing my waterfall, I planned to use lights in the water and the garden surrounding its lower pond. We have a great view of this area from both outside the house and a sunroom. It would be very inconvenient to run outside to turn the lights on and off. Instead they are wired directly to a switch in the kitchen. Now when I go to bed, I can easily turn the lights off without going outside.

Will you want to add a waterfall in the future? What about a fountain? If you think you might add these later, it is best to plan the electrical source now. If you use heavy equipment to dig the pond, the same excavator can dig trenches for the electrical lines and conduit can be put in place. This is much cheaper than doing it as a separate job in the future. It also means your lawn or garden will only be ripped up once.

Both solar and wind can be used at the pond to generate electricity, and these may be very good options if the pond is some distance from the home. These are detailed in the chapter called Large-scale Ponds.

Size

Deciding on the size of the pond will be the most crucial, and probably the most difficult, decision you make. Unless you are creating an earth pond with no liner, it is a decision that can't easily be changed. Once the pond is complete, it is almost impossible to enlarge or reduce it.

A good place to start is by visiting existing ponds on lots the same size as yours. This will give you the best perspective of how big the pond should be. Most owners will be quite happy talking to you and showing off their pond.

Many cities have annual garden tours that let you visit owners' backyards and see their ponds. Some larger cities will even have tours featuring only gardens with water features. You can also look at pictures in books and online, but these will rarely give you a good perspective about the size of the pond relative to that of the property. You really need to see the pond in its surroundings.

As a general guide, I can state that you will always wish you had made it bigger. Larger ponds are more enjoyable and easier to maintain. However, your pond should look as if it fits into your yard. If you convert your whole backyard into a pond, it may look out of place. However, I know of one local pond and waterfall that takes up the whole backyard, and it is very impressive.

A larger pond costs more to dig the hole, get rid of the soil, and buy the liner. Purchased stones can add significantly to the expense. A larger surface area results in more evaporation, which requires more water, and in some locations, this can be a significant yearly cost. Plants are also more expensive, but you can always start with a small number and let them multiply naturally. It is easier to maintain a balanced ecosystem in a larger pond.

The natural pond design used in this book uses large planting shelves, compared to a standard pond. These shelves will take up one-third to one-half of the surface area and will make the pond look smaller than it is. A pond that is 10 × 10 feet, or 100 square feet, will only have about 55 square feet of open water. If you want 100 square feet of open water, you will have to build it 200 square feet.

Have you designed the rest of the garden? If you start with a grassy backyard and little in the way of landscaping, you may find it difficult to decide on the size of the pond. It is best to design the whole backyard as a single project. This allows you to understand how you will use the whole space and how much space to allocate to a pond. If you want to add a vegetable garden, a tool shed, and a patio, you might have automatically determined its allocated space. All of these landscape projects don't have to be done simultaneously, but knowing the full plan will help you make the right decisions in sizing and placing your pond.

Depth

Shallow ponds heat up faster, which can be a problem for some types of fish. Goldfish and koi prefer cooler water. Warm water also encourages more algae growth. For these and other reasons, I recommend a depth of at least two feet deep; three feet is much better.

In cold climates, the pond may be covered with a full sheet of ice in winter. As the temperature drops, the ice thickens, mostly in a downward direction. Prolonged cold weather results in thicker ice and less water under the ice. You would think the pond would freeze solid fairly easily in zone 5 and colder areas, but there is also a warming factor. The center of the Earth is warm, and that warmth moves through the soil to the surface. In effect, there is a small heater at the bottom of the pond, the soil, which slows down the rate of freezing. A pond that is two feet deep will rarely freeze solid, except in extremely cold climates.

How thick will the ice get where you live? That is a difficult question to answer. The rate of ice thickening depends on temperature, wind, snow cover, and the current thickness of ice. Thick ice gets thicker more slowly than thin ice, and a cover of snow slows the process even more. As temperatures get near freezing, the ice gets thinner; on mild winter days, you actually loose ice. A more detailed discussion on how ice thickens is provided in the References section.

As a general guide, you can use the following information. It represents ice growth without the protection of snow.

Development of ice as a function of temperature and time

Average temperature (°F)	Inches of ice growth in a week
30	2
25	4
20	6
10	10
0	12
−20	16

Source: lakeice.squarespace.com/ice-growth/

Water Source

After filling your pond the first time, you will probably need to top it up occasionally. Having easy access to water is a huge advantage. How will you fill the pond? In most backyards, you can easily run a garden hose from the house to the pond. With normal water pressure, you should be able to reach 1,000 feet with a ⅝-inch ID hose.

My previous house was on a normal-sized lot, and every couple of weeks, I would drag hoses all around the garden—it was always a lot of work. At my current house, I decided right from the start to lay some underground water lines. They are wonderful to use. If you are starting a landscape project, I would strongly recommend them. Have a tap in each garden and one near the pond. Ideally you want to reach the pond with one garden hose.

There are other sources of water to consider. Collecting rain water is not only cost-effective but also environmentally sound. Your roof collects quite a bit of rain, which can be used to top up your pond. Set up a series of barrels to collect the rain or run a line directly from the downspouts to the pond. An alternative is to make the pond an integral part of a rain garden. This is detailed in the chapter Pools, Bogs, and Rain Gardens.

Bogs and Rain Gardens

Sloped ground can also be used to fill your pond. A hill or sloped area will have water runoff during a heavy rain that will follow the contours of your property to the lowest point. By locating the pond there, it will fill naturally each time it rains. However, this low spot can also cause a big problem. What happens if there is too much rain and the pond overfills? This is easily prevented by adding a spillway that will carry excess water away from the pond, provided it has some place to go.

Do you have a natural spring on your property? The water from this can be used to fill the pond, but do not build it on top of the spring. In this location, water comes up under the liner, which just does not work. A better setup is to locate the pond downhill and let the spring run into it. Alternatively, you might be able to add a pump to supply spring water to the pond.

Trees

Trees and ponds do not get along very well. Tree roots, which are mostly in the top six to eight inches of soil, are located much farther from the tree than most people realize. The old rule of thumb was that most feeder roots are at the drip line, the edge of the leaves, but we now know that they extend two or even three times this distance from the trunk of the tree. If you damage too many roots when excavating, you will harm or even kill the tree. How much is too much? That is really hard to say. It depends on the type of tree, age, and soil conditions. An arborist may be able to answer this, but they might not have much experience digging holes near trees. As a general rule, damage no more than one-quarter of the root system.

Trees cause another problem for ponds—they drop leaves. Even evergreen trees lose needles every year. The leaves falling into the pond add organic matter and put a strain on the balanced ecosystem. Some people recommend that ponds should not be placed near trees, and that certainly solves the problem. Others cover the pond in fall with netting to keep most leaves out. This works, but looks ugly and is extra work. In my experience, a properly planted natural pond can handle some leaves with no problem. A heavy load of leaves might need to be scooped out in fall.

Trees near the pond will make it look more natural. From a purely aesthetic point of view, they contribute a lot to the pond, so try to have some nearby. If you don't have any, consider planting one or more on the north side of the pond.

The natural pond works because of all the plants, and most like lots of sun. For example, water lilies will not bloom without at least six hours of sun a day. Too many trees cause too much shade, especially on the south side. Locate your pond so that it gets at least six hours of direct sun, and keep in mind that trees grow. How much shade will you have in five and ten years?

Pond Liners

There are basically three ways to create the bottom of a pond. Dig a hole, and let the natural soil create a seal to retain water. If your soil is suitable for holding water, this is a cheap and simple method. To determine if this will work, you will need to test your soil. This is detailed in the next chapter. The other two methods use a man-made material to keep the water in place: a rigid preformed liner or a flexible rubber liner

Preformed liners, hard plastic shells that are completely formed into the final shape of the pond, are available in various sizes for small and mid-sized ponds but not for large ponds. They are easier to install than a flexible liner, and you know exactly what the final pond will look like before you buy it. This convenience is balanced by the fact that you usually can't have the exact shape you want. The natural pond design requires large planting shelves, and most preformed liners do not have them.

Preformed liners (figure 16) are a good choice for your first pond if you want to keep things simple, but the serious pond gardener will be much happier with a flexible liner. These can be used to make small ponds and can be joined together to make any size. Since the liner is flexible, it can also be formed into any desired shape, and installation is only marginally more difficult than a preformed liner.

Human Access

The best way to enjoy your pond is to get close to the water. Many people like to sit right by the pond and daydream. You also need access, ideally on all sides, for doing maintenance on the plants.

Your design needs to include access to the pond. Will you have a patio next to it, or will there be a lawn? Will this access be on one side with plantings on the other three sides? How do you get from other key areas in your garden to the pond? If you come out of your back door and want to visit the pond, what kind of path will lead to the pond? Think about all of these questions as you select your location and start formalizing your design.

Because the path to the pond will be used quite a bit, it should be a significant part of your overall garden design and integrated into the pond design. Consider using the same material for this path as you have for others in the garden to create one cohesive landscape.

FIGURE 11
A dock provides easy
access to the pond.
This view shows the
back to the teahouse
pictured in figure 10.

Think about accessing the actual edge of the water. The edge on most sides will consist of rocks that cover and hide the liner but are not easy to walk on. Some options to consider for the access point include a patio, a sandy beach, a dock, or even a bridge. A sandy beach is a nice feature on a larger pond, especially if you plan to swim in it. This also makes it easy for wildlife like small birds to come to the edge for a drink.

A bridge or dock can also add interest to the pond and garden. They offer a different outlook over the pond, more directly into the water, which is great for viewing fish. The dock shown in figures 10 and 11 crosses the pond, so that when you are standing on it, you don't see the edge below the dock. The advantage of this design is that all four footings are outside of the pond liner, making construction a bit easier. In figure 28, the dock juts out over the water and also has all footings located outside of the pond liner. Alternatively, this dock could have been built with the two front footings in the water, using the construction methods described in chapter five.

FIGURE 12
A bridge provides good viewing points for wildlife.

It is essential to design the access points before construction starts, especially if you are adding bridges or docks, since they might change how you create the pond.

Rocks

Most of the rocks that are used to hide the liner will eventually be hidden by plants, so their selection is not that critical. However, they will look best if they are roundish, without sharp edges, and don't look man-made. Select some that are local to your area for a more natural look.

Choose rocks in various sizes from small to as large as you can handle. There is nothing as impressive as some very large rocks around a pond. A few good-sized ones will also be used inside the pond for aesthetic reasons. It is nice to have a few special rocks beside a beach area since it will be open and not hidden behind plants.

Although rocks can be expensive and you will need more than antici-pated, in most areas of the country, they are easy to scrounge. Start by looking around your own property for some you can use. If your soil is naturally rocky, you will be getting a lot out of your excavation, but you will probably still need more. Start collecting them as soon as you begin planning a pond. Construction sites will usually let you take all the rocks you want. Farms and neighbor gardens may also have rocks they want to get rid of. Check the classified sections in newspapers and online. Anyone who doesn't want the rocks will be happy to have you carry them away. However, rocks do belong to someone, and just because they are sitting along the side of the road does not mean they are yours for the taking. Always ask permission. Don't take rocks from natural habitats because they are vital for wildlife.

Shape of the Pond and Planting Shelves

Since the pond liner is either a square or rectangle, it naturally forms a circle or oval pond. Neither of these shapes is very natural looking. You could make an irregular-shaped pond, but that wastes a lot of liner. The best way to solve this problem is to make an oval pond with irregularly shaped planting shelves. Add wider shelves in some areas and narrower in others. The final apparent shape of the pond will follow the outline of the open water, not the actual shape of the edge. Once the plants are established, the pond will look irregular and natural.

Planting shelves should be equal to one-third to one-half of the total pond size.

Shelves that contain plants of different heights around the edge will also make the pond look less regular and more natural. Putting the right plants in the right places can also hide unwanted views behind the pond or expose desirable views. Stand at your main access point and decide where you want more or fewer plants. Then plan to have wider shelves where you want the most plants. You probably don't want plants at your main access point because they reduce the view of the water. For the same reason, a beach area is usually designed without plants.

Adding some strategically placed larger rocks both around the perimeter of the pond and directly in the water will also change the perceived shape of the pond. A dock, bridge, or beach access point changes the view even more.

FIGURE 13
The irregular shape of planting shelves hides the unnatural looking oval pond.

Plants

At this stage of planning, it is not essential to select the type of plants you will use, but there are some decisions you should make now. Most water plants will grow fine on the planting shelves in a few inches of water.

Water lilies are vital to the pond and need to be treated differently. They grow on the bottom of the pond and need a particular depth to grow properly. Figure out where to plant them at an appropriate depth. Small and medium-sized water lilies require one to two feet. Large ones thrive at two to three feet but should only be planted in ponds with more than 200 square feet of surface area.

There are two options for accommodating water lilies. You can create special planting shelves at the right depth, or you can make the pond deeper and then add some material that will create an artificial shelf. For example, cement blocks on the bottom of the pond could alter a four-foot-deep pond and raise large water lilies up to three feet. If you want to use planting shelves, plan their location and depth before you do any digging.

It is usually best to keep the water lilies away from the viewing area so they don't block the view into the water. They also don't like moving water, so plant them away from any inlet, waterfall, or fountain.

Start giving some thought to the plants that will be planted around the outside of the pond. Will these be short plants or tall? Are you trying to hide some views or open them up? Is the soil suitable or do you need to bring in some new top soil? What is the slope of the land surrounding the pond? Is it level or does it slope away from the pond? You might be able to use some of the excavated soil to fix a slope problem. It is easier to plant on level ground or a gentle slope.

Excavated Soil

Digging the hole for the pond will produce more soil than you think. What are you going to do with it? The excavated material is probably going to be poor, sub-soil quality. If you use this to level the garden, plan to top it with at least six inches of good top soil, which will make plants grow much better.

Is your property sloped? The excess soil can be used to level another part of the garden or allow you to build the pond on a slope. This will be discussed in more detail in the next chapter. If you can't use the extra soil, it will need to be removed from the site, adding cost to the project. Check on free selling sites, like Craigslist, and you may find someone to take it away for free.

CHAPTER 5

Building

Previous chapters have provided information that will help you design your pond. By now you have gone through a planning process and know where you are going to put the pond, and you have made drawings to show its size and shape. This chapter will discuss the practical aspects of construction. It is almost time to start digging.

Site Evaluation

Before you start digging, it is critical to check for utility lines such as electric, gas, telecommunications, and water. Most communities provide an inspection of your property, usually free, and make sure there are no buried services where you will be digging. If utility lines are found near the planned site, you may have to change the location. If you don't want to do that, talk to the utility company and see if they are able to move the line.

The next step is to check that the site is level. Because water is always level, ponds need an edge at the same height all the way around, or the water will run out on the low side. Don't try to eyeball the level of the ground because people are not very good at seeing a small slope—you have to measure it.

FIGURE 14
Measuring the slope
of your property.

Take a two-by-four board that is about ten feet long and make sure it is straight. Longer is better, but a very long board becomes hard to handle unless you have help. Mark a point at approximately the middle of the pond. You don't have to be too accurate. Set one end of the board at this point, and lay it on the ground on the two-inch wide part. Place a spirit level on top and raise the low end until the board is level. Use a tape measure to determine the height between the bottom of the board and the ground, as shown in figure 14. If your pond is wider than the length of this board, move it to the end of the first measurement, and repeat the process. In this way, you can use a ten-foot board and measure the slope over a long distance.

Measure the slope over the entire pond area. If the slope over the whole pond area is not more than about six inches per ten feet, don't worry about the slope. You can easily correct a small slope after excavating. If the slope is more than six inches, take a step back and do some more design work.

There are several ways to deal with a larger slope. You can solve the problem by choosing a different location that is flatter. You can also plan to raise the low end of the ground so that you end up with a level area. Remember that you will have lots of extra soil to deal with as you dig the

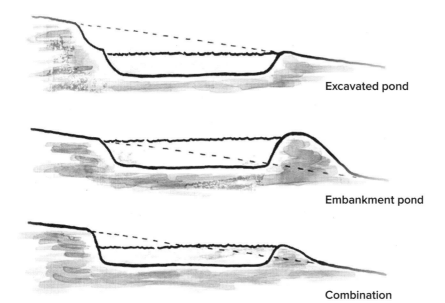

Excavated pond

Embankment pond

Combination

FIGURE 15
Building a pond
on sloped ground.

pit and using it to solve a slope problem eliminates or at least reduces the problem of disposing of it.

Raising one end by one or two feet is easily done, but if you need to go any higher, it is crucial to construct the embankment wall correctly to support the water. Building such dams is discussed more fully in the chapter on large-scale ponds.

Another alternative to correct a slope is to lower the high end. This might be the best solution if the edge of the pond is being built into a hill, as shown in figure 6. You can carve out part of the hill so that the previous high spot is now level with the low spot. This solution does require more digging, but from a structural point of view, it makes for stronger side walls since the soil is not disturbed. The hill side should be leveled to a spot at least two feet past the edge of the pond so that any erosion on the hill will not empty into the pond.

Review your design and plan to solve any slope problem before you start digging. The final pond will need to be level all around the edge.

Soil Type

The type of soil can influence the construction method you use. Is a pond liner required? Lots of people want to build a pond without a liner since it is less expensive. If your soil has a high clay content, the clay holds the water in place and you might not need a liner.

If you want to consider building the pond without a liner, dig a hole to a depth equal to the final pond. The best place to do this is in the middle of the future pond. Fill the hole with water and wait to see what happens. It will probably run away, so fill it again. If on the second fill the water does not run away, you might be able to skip the liner.

Ponds that don't use a liner will always seep some water into the surrounding soil. A high clay content in your soil will reduce the amount of such seepage. Natural ponds without a liner usually have a water source that fills them to overcome the seepage. I will discuss more about such earth-lined ponds in the chapter on large-scale ponds. The rest of this chapter will assume you are using a liner.

Soil type also affects the shape of the pond walls. Sandy soil is not very stable, and as you dig in it, the sides of the hole will tend to collapse. This soil requires sides that have a very gradual slope to prevent them from collapsing. In clay soil, which does not have this problem, the sides of your pond can be much more vertical.

How much slope is enough? That is really hard to answer because it depends on the soil type and every soil is different. In my soil, which is about 40 percent clay, I can dig almost vertical sides with no collapse, even when the pit sits empty for two years. You need to use a slope that allows the side of the pond to stay in place all on its own.

A simple way to determine the amount of clay in soil is by adding some soil to water and watching it settle. A video describing this method is listed in the References section.

Installing a Preformed Pond

A preformed pond is a plastic shell that has been molded into the shape of a pond. One advantage of using this type of pond is that the installation

is easier. A disadvantage is that, being limited to the available shapes, you can't design the pond the way you want. Although ponds do have planting shelves, many don't have enough to make a natural pond work properly.

Set the preformed pond in its final location, open side up, and orient it the way you want. Lay a board across the top of the pond and use a spirit level to make sure it is sitting level. If not, add some bits of wood or soil underneath to make it level. Then take a plumb and mark the edge of the pond on the ground. Take some wooden stakes or landscapers' paint and mark a line that is 12 inches beyond the edge of the pond.

Dig out the pond edge by following the marked line. Continue digging a hole in the shape of the pond, making sure that any shelves remain in the pit. The bottom should be dug six inches deeper than the final level of the installed pond. Place the pond form into the hole from time to time to make sure the pit is dug correctly. Once finished, you should have

FIGURE 16
Preformed ponds.

FIGURE 17
Installing a
preformed pond.

six-inch gap between the soil and the pond on all sides, below planting shelves, and below the bottom of the pond. This will be filled with sand to make a good fit between the soil and the pond.

Add builders' sand to the lowest point of the pit and pack it down with a tamper or a two-by-four board until the pond sits on this sand layer and is at the right height. Then repeat the process for any horizontal shelves in the mold.

Place the pond into the pit and check that the edge is level in all directions. If it is not, take the pond back out and adjust the sand layers until it is level. Don't rush this step of the process. You might need to take the pond out a half dozen times to get it right.

Once the pond is level and positioned correctly, start filling it with water. As it rises in the pond, add sand around the outside. If you can reach the area, compact the sand with a 2-by-4, but don't over-compact. You don't want to push sand under the pond and raise it up. You also don't want to push in the sides of the pond, although the rising water should prevent this from happening. Pour water around the outside of the pond into the fresh sand to help compact it.

FIGURE 18
Supporting
the edge of a
preformed pond.

Slowly work your way up the side of the pond, adding some water inside, some sand outside, and some water outside. Keep an eye on the spirit level to make sure the pond does not shift. If it does, you will need to start over. Continue this process until the sand is right up to the rim of the pond.

The edge of the preformed pond is not very strong. If you have an area where you will be walking right up to the edge, reinforce this by placing flat stones or bricks under the pond to provide extra support, as shown in figure 18. These can then be covered with other material to hide the edge on the pond.

Flexible Pond Liners

Flexible pond liners are available in a number of different materials including plastics and rubber. Some people even use cheap vapor barrier plastic, normally used to seal your home, but don't do it. Building a pond is a lot of work, and the last thing you want is to redo it because you got a hole in some cheaper material.

The best material for the job and the only one I would recommend is 45 mil EPDM rubber.

Although available in several thicknesses, 45 mil is the standard for ponds. The rubber is also used for sealing industrial roofs and may be cheaper when bought at a roofing supply company, but this rubber is not guaranteed to be "fish safe." Is there really a difference between the

EPDM sold for roofing and the one sold for ponds? I don't know, but why take a chance to save a few cents?

Buy your liner from a dealer who specializes in ponds. Most nurseries sell pond liners, and there are a numerous online sources as well. When comparing prices, be aware that pond liners are very heavy and shipping can add significantly to the cost of online shopping. Nurseries usually have a spring sale on liners when the demand is high and another sale in fall to get rid of leftover stock.

A rubber liner weighs about 0.3 pounds per square foot. A pond that is 10-by-20-by-4 feet will require a liner that is 600 square feet, which weighs 180 pounds. Liners are available in widths of 10, 15, 20, 25, 30, 40, and 50 feet and lengths of 50 and 100 feet. The length is usually cut to your specifications—you don't need to buy 50 feet. Local nurseries generally carry only a few of these widths and will cut to length. Larger online sources can supply any of the sizes listed and will also cut to length.

Any size of pond can be lined with a rubber liner. It can be cut fairly easily with a knife and joined together to fit very large ponds. Liners are available in standard widths, so it is cost-effective to design your pond to match available sizes. If you design your pond so that it needs an 11-foot liner, you will have to buy one that is 15 feet wide and waste much of your liner. At about $1 per square foot, this can add up quickly.

How much liner do you need? It is fairly easy to calculate by following these steps. Measure the width (W) of the pond at its widest part and the length (L) at the longest point. Figure 19 shows you how to measure an irregular-shaped pond.

Measure the depth (D) of the pond from the top of the soil to the deepest part of the pit. Ignore planting shelves. The liner needs to go above the waterline and over the edge of the pond, so you need to measure the soil height, not the water height.

Decide on how much overhang you want. This is the extra liner that goes over the top edge of the pond. For small ponds that are less than 30-by-30 feet, a one-foot overhang on each side is sufficient. For larger ponds, add a two-foot overhang.

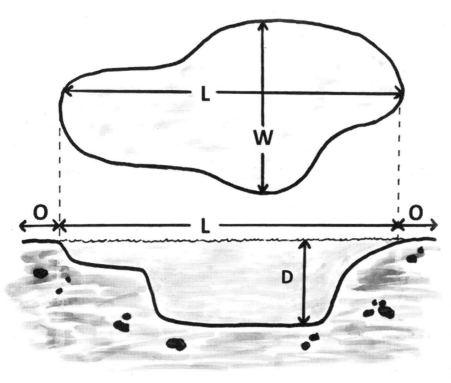

FIGURE 19
Calculating the size of liner required (L=Length, W=Width, D=Depth, and O=Overhang.)

Calculate the size of the required liner as follows:

Width of liner = Width (W) + 2 times the Overhang (O) + 2 times the Depth (D)

Length of liner = Length (L) + 2 times the Overhang (O) + 2 times the Depth (D)

Digging the Hole for a Flexible Liner

There are two fundamental ways to dig the hole, by hand or with machinery. Digging by hand simply requires a good spade, a wheelbarrow, and a good back. It can be a lot of work, but it will allow you to carefully sculpt the shelves as needed.

An excavator can dig a 40-foot pond in an hour or two, which makes this option very attractive. But there are some things to consider before going this route. It can be expensive. The machine you select needs to be able to get to the pond location. In some cases, there may not be enough room between the houses. Removing part of a fence might make this work.

The soil that is removed from the hole still has to be dealt with. An excavator is efficient at digging the hole, but it is slow for moving the soil to the front of the house. A bobcat is better at moving soil, but they are not as good for digging. You might need two different machines to get the job done.

Is it better to rent the machines and do it yourself or hire someone? You can certainly rent the machines for the day, and they are not difficult to use. You will be slow at first, but after an hour or two, you will get the hang of it. It is also a lot of fun if you have never done this before. However, you will probably find that hiring someone with the machines will cost the same as renting the machines, and they will get the job done faster.

The machine can only dig part of the hole. It is not accurate enough to delicately cut out the planting shelves and slope the sides properly. The fine-tuning is best done manually with a shovel.

The first step in digging the hole is to remove the sod, weeds, and topsoil. Remove this top layer to a point that is several feet past the planned edge of the pond to make it easier to work on the pond. Don't discard topsoil or mix it with the lower levels of soil because this valuable resource can be used later to landscape the surrounding area or elsewhere around the garden.

The next step is to level the site so that the edge of the pond is level to about six inches. Don't worry about being too exact, since you will be able to adjust this later in the building process.

A pool created on sloped land will need to have the soil from the high point moved to the low point. The soil being added to any low point must be compacted as you go, so it does not shift or settle later. Move six inches of soil and compact it with a tamper or with the excavator. For a large area, you can rent a motorized tamper. Once the soil is compact, repeat the process with another six inches of soil.

When the site is level, mark out the perimeter of the pond with land-scapers' paint or simply insert some pegs every two feet or so. This does not have to be too precise.

Digging the hole for the pond is similar to carving a piece of wood. You take off larger pieces first and then slowly remove more wood to add the fine details. If you take too much off, the carving is ruined because you can't put the wood back. The same applies to a pond. Dig slowly to get a basic shape and then fine-tune things. Be careful not to remove soil that is needed. You want to use the existing compacted soil to form the hole. Putting loose soil back along the sides or to add a planting shelf does not work for most soil. It is just not stable enough.

After marking the outline of the pond, take your design and divide it into horizontal layers. The first layer will probably be the top planting shelves. These will be about eight inches or so below grade. Dig the pond to this level. The edges for this level can be fairly steep since they will be covered with rock eventually. If you are making a beach area, use a more gradual slope.

When the first level is complete, outline the next, which might be the lower planting shelves for the water lilies. Dig out this level, making sure to slope the sides so that the walls are stable. It is a good idea for now to leave them sloped more than you want. You can always increase the slope later but you can't decrease it easily.

If your plan includes some steps to allow you to enter the pond, carve them in at the right spot out of compact native soil so they hold their shape.

Continue digging out the hole one level at a time.

Figure 20 shows the finished dug hole. The soil here dries into very hard clumps, making it difficult to get a smooth finish. However, it contains virtually no rocks, which makes digging easier, provided the soil is moist. The sides of the pond have a very gradual slope that made it easy

FIGURE 20
A pond that has been dug out. Notice the large planting shelf in the middle of the picture.

to dig with an excavator. My pond was dug mostly by hand, and I used much steeper sides. Both methods will work.

Rocks can be a big problem as you dig the hole. When you encounter a rock, you'll have to decide what to do about it. If it is in the middle of the pond, just remove it. You will need a lot of rocks of all sizes to finish the pond, so separate them from the soil as you dig and create a pile near the pond.

When you encounter rocks near the wall of the pond, you need to be more careful. Small ones can be removed. Removing larger ones may cause the wall to collapse, making the pond bigger than you want or making the slope of the wall unstable. Deciding if you should remove a rock depends on its size and the stability of the soil. The wall does not have to be absolutely flat. Round rocks that stick out a bit are not a problem since they are easily covered with the liner. It is usually best to remove rocks that have a sharp edge.

When I had almost finished hand digging my first pond, I encountered a huge rock at the bottom. It was too big to lift out, and the sides were too steep to roll it out. While I was thinking of renting a sledgehammer, the solution popped into my head: I dug deeper beside the rock and rolled it into the hole. It is still at the bottom of the pond.

Don't dig the hole larger than the liner you plan to use; keep measuring as you dig. If it gets too big, the easiest way to fix the problem is to add some soil to the bottom of the hole, but that reduces your depth.

Here is an easy way to measure the hole. Cut a string to the length of the pond liner and another to the width. Take the string for the width and lay it on the soil following the contour of the hole at the widest part of the pond. You should have excess string sticking out at both ends, representing the overhang. Repeat this with the string for the length.

Preparing the Hole

The hole you have dug should now look just like the shape of the final pond. You have finished any final adjustments, and the pond size is correct. The next step is to prepare the hole for the liner.

Go over all of the soil that will come in contact with the liner and cut off all tree roots. Large roots should be cut flush with a saw; for small one, use a wire side cutter or hand pruner. Ensure that no sharp edges stick out. If possible, cut them just below soil level. Then remove all sharp stones from inside the pond.

If you are adding a bridge or dock with footings in the water, make sure the soil under them is well compacted to prevent any future settling. Take extra care to compact the area and add extra soil if needed to raise it to the level of the rest of the pond floor. The method for building the footings is described later in this chapter.

The next step is to put a protective layer all over the soil, including the side walls, creating an underlayment to prevent any punctures to the liner from below. Companies selling pond liners will also sell a protective fabric material for this purpose. In my experience, this material is very thin and does not give me much confidence that it will protect the liner from a sharp stone. Some pond books recommend using sand, which works quite well on flat surfaces, but it is useless for covering the sides of the pond. Some people recommend newspaper—I'm not sure why. Will newspaper stop a sharp rock?

I prefer to use old carpet. Most of the carpet produced in North America is synthetic plastic that lasts a long time under a liner. After ten years, the carpet under my waterfall looks as good as new. Although any synthetic carpet will do, some are easier to work with than others. Low pile carpet is easier to work with than high plush and will provide just as good a protection. Carpet is fairly easy to cut by turning it over and cutting the back layer with a utility knife. Some cut cleaner than others, so try and find ones that cut well, so you don't become frustrated with all of the loose threads sticking out.

If your friends or family are not replacing their carpet, visit a dealer. They need to discard the old carpet removed from installations and are only too happy to give it to you instead of paying dumping fees. One dealer in my area puts it a dumpster, and you can help yourself. Make sure you remove old staples and nails.

Carpet is fairly stiff and thick, which makes it hard to line a round pond. It works best to cut the carpet into strips and then lay them over-lapped, plush side up or down; it does not really matter. Use wider strips in straight sections and narrow strips around curves. It is easier to lay the carpet than to put the instructions into words. Your goal is to cover all of the soil under the liner. Overlap the joints by several inches so that no bare soil shows.

Laying the carpet on the vertical walls can be tricky if the slope is very steep. The best approach is to cut long strips that will cover all of the way from the edge of the pond to the bottom of the pond. Then hold these in place with rocks along the top edge. These rocks will not be in the way

FIGURE 21
The carpet underlay will help protect the liner.

as you position the liner and start filling the pond. Once the liner is in place and has water in the bottom, remove the rocks and the carpet will stay in place.

At this point, your neighbors will think you are a little crazy. Just tell them that carpet in the backyard is the new in thing in garden design.

Installing the Pond Liner

Installing the pond liner may seem like a daunting task, but it is easier than you think if you follow some simple suggestions. Rubber gets stiff when it is cold, so lay it out flat on the grass so that the sun can warm it, which makes it much easier to work with.

The liner is quite tough, and it takes quite a bit of force to puncture it, but you don't want to take any chances. Whenever you walk on it, either remove your shoes or wear soft-sole ones. It is really hard to step on a sharp stone wearing only socks.

The liner is quite heavy, which makes it hard to get into place. A wheelbarrow is great for moving it to the edge of the pond. Then roll it into the pit, making sure not to disturb the underlayment. There is no up or down side on the liner, so put into place either way. Once it is in the bottom of the hole, position the center of the liner in the right spot. If it is too far to one side, you will have too much liner on one side and not enough on the other. This is one reason why you added the extra overhang to your measurements. Unroll the liner and lay it loosely in place. Try to get it as flat as possible on the bottom and sides. Don't worry about folds at this point. Your only goal is to position the center of the liner in the right spot.

For large liners, it is easier to work in one direction at a time. Roll out the width and get it positioned correctly. Then repeat the process for the length. Because of the weight, you might have to roll part of it up again to facilitate moving. While you are getting the liner centered in the pond, check the edges. There should be a one- or two-foot overhang, depending on your design. You should actually see more than this, since the liner will settle as the water pulls it into the pond. If you don't have enough liner around the edge, now is the time to correct the problem.

There are several ways to fix a liner that is too short. You can add more soil into the bottom of the hole. This needs to be done beneath the underlayment. Every inch of soil added will add two inches along the top—one inch on each side. You can also lower the edge of the pond. Another option is to bring in the sides of the top edge, reducing the circumference of the pond. This only works where you have planting shelves.

Footings for a Dock or Bridge

Docks and bridges can be built so that none of the supports are in the water, as shown in figures 10, 11, and 28. If you don't have footings in the water, you can skip this section.

Footings in the water can provide extra support, but they need to be added at this point in the project. They are made from large flat material placed over the liner. The supporting posts sit on these footings. You can create the footings using poured concrete, but this is more work than is normally required. A simpler option is to use flat patio stones. The 2-by-2-foot squares provide a large surface area to distribute the extra weight and are easy to move around.

Locate the position for the footings and add two layers of underlayment on top of the liner. These can be an inch or two bigger than the patio stones. Then place the patio stones on top of the underlayment. This will prevent any punctures in the liner from the stones.

FIGURE 22
Footings for the bridge shown in figure 13.

If more height is required, stack several patio stones or place bricks on top of the patio stone. This same setup can be used to add raised shelves for water lilies or create a permanent island in the middle of the pond. The key is to add puncture protection between the footings and the liner.

Adding Water

When you are certain that the center of the liner is in the right position, and all footings are in place, start adding water. It is much easier to stretch the liner and make folds with water in the pond. There are two reasons for this. First, the weight of the water holds the liner in place. Even a small amount allows you to pull fairly hard on the liner without fear of moving the bottom of it out of place. Second, as water fills the pond, it stretches and settles the liner tight against the underlayment. This stretching will change any folds placed high above the waterline. You will find that it is easier to make most folds at or near the waterline. Once the fold is made, the water pressure holds it in place.

As water fills the pond, pull the liner tight to remove any wrinkles. If you get to a point where you can't get the wrinkle out, add a fold. Folds need to be made in any area where the pond is round. Making the folds is much like wrapping a Christmas present. Tuck in the excess rubber, so that you create neat folds that lie flat against the side of the pond. When done correctly, you will see the fold, but it will not stick up into the water. Try to add as few folds as possible to give a neat flat look to the pond. One larger fold is better than two small ones, but don't follow this rule religiously. Some people recommend gluing the folds so they are closed to organic matter. That is not necessary, and it is a lot of extra work.

If your plan involves moving water from a stream or waterfall, it is advisable to make the folds so that they point away from the moving water. In this way, the moving water keeps the folds closed instead of pushing water under them and opening them.

The folds will look ugly as you are making them because they are very visible. In two months, they will be covered with microbes and hardly noticeable. You just have to have faith that they will disappear.

Protecting Planting Shelves

There are two types of planting shelves. One is a lower planting shelf that holds pots for deep-water plants like water lilies. These are not very heavy and are not likely to poke holes in the liner. These shelves do not need further protection. In a shallow pond, you may not have this shelf because the water lilies can sit right on the bottom.

The other type of shelf is the main planting area around the perimeter of the pond. They will be covered with rocks, and if you step on the rocks while placing or maintaining the plants, you could poke a hole in the liner. For this reason, I strongly suggest that you add extra protection to these areas.

The best way to protect the liner from stones sitting on it is to add an overlayment, which can be the same material as the underlayment.

FIGURE 23
Carpet has been used as the overlayment to prevent punctures from above the liner.

I prefer to place carpet on top of the liner anywhere you will be adding stones on top of the liner. All of this overlayment will be covered with stones.

Follow the exact same procedure for the overlayment as for the underlayment. Work in smaller strips and overlap pieces after most of the pond liner folds are in place, but before the water level reaches the planting shelves. You won't be able to change the folds after the carpet is in place.

The pond shown in figure 23 is mostly finished. Water is being added, the overlayment is in place, and most of the stones are in place. You will notice that the liner at the top center of the picture is not protected with overlayment. This area will not require stones because the finished pond (figure 28) will have a dock covering this part of the liner.

Stones for the Planting Shelf

Once the overlayment is in place, you can start placing stones on the planting shelf. Figure 24 is a cross-section of a pond showing the arrangement of stones for the shelf on the left and the beach area on the right.

Start by making a ring of large stones along the inner edge of the shelf. You want to select ones with flat bottoms and a fair amount of weight so

FIGURE 24
Cross-section of a pond showing the planting shelves on the left and the beach area on the right.

that they will not roll into the bottom of the pond. For aesthetic reasons, vary their size; otherwise it will look like a ring of stones that is not very natural. As the water level goes down in summer, a few of the larger ones will pop up above the water level, while most will still be submerged. It is quite acceptable to have a few that sit above the water level even when the pond is full.

Incorporate some larger display rocks that sit on either the beach area or a planting shelf, so that most are above the waterline. These serve no useful purpose except to make the pond look much more natural. If you

FIGURE 25
Partially completed planting shelves.

add more than one, make sure to vary their size and shape. Too many will take up too much planting space, and they'll look unnatural. Figure 24 shows two such rocks. Let your creative juices flow for this job.

If your planting shelves are very wide, you might also want to add some flat rocks right in the planting area to provide places to stand while maintaining the plants. Keep in mind that every stepping stone reduces the space for plants in the pond, and you want as many plants as possible.

The next job is to put a ring of larger rocks around the outer edge of the planting shelf to give you a stable base for laying the stones that will hide the edge of the pond. In the finished pond, plants will hide most of these stones. The stones need to be big enough to support the rocks above them, but otherwise they can be any size or shape. It is a good place to use up your ugly rocks.

You have now created the inside and outside edge of the planting shelf, which is clearly visible in figure 25 as two rows of large rocks. It is time to fill the space between these rocks with small stones. A few have already been added in figure 25. These stones will give plants something to attach their roots to and provide a lot of surface area for microbes to live. You won't see them in the finished pond, so don't worry about their look or shape. Smaller is better since small ones provide a larger total surface area. I like to repurpose all of the small stones I rake out of my various gardens. Add them to a depth of at least two inches. Make sure you do not go as high as the stones on the inner edge of the shelf, or else they will fall into the bottom of the pond. The top part of figure 25 shows a planting shelf with all of the rocks in place.

Leveling the Pond Edge

As water fills the pond, it will be very easy for you to see how level your pond edge is. If it looks as if water will overflow at one spot, then you need to fix this low point. Either add soil under the underlayment to raise the low spot, or take soil away from the high spots. As water fills the pond, just keep walking around it and increase or decrease the height of problem areas.

As you level the pond, take notice of the amount of liner that is sticking up and over the edge. You want some liner above the final high waterline. If it is a bit short, you will need to decrease the height of the edge around the whole pond. If there is too much liner, you can decide to cut off the excess or raise the height of the pond.

Adding the Spillway

A spillway should be added to control the flow of excess water. As you are leveling the edge and adding more water, start putting the spillway in place.

FIGURE 26
The spillway controls where overflow water will go.

The spillway is a section of the pond where the edge is lower than every other point. It should be at least two feet wide; four feet is better for a larger pond. The low spot of the spillway should be four inches below the top edge of the pond.

Remove the soil from under the underlayment so that the level of the spillway is at the correct height. The water level of the pond will never go higher than the height of the spillway. It should slope away from the pond and extend several feet from the edge. It is critical that any water running along it can't run under the pond liner.

Cover the spillway with some excess liner, which you can cut from the surplus overhang at round sections of the pond. Underlayment and overlayment are not needed here, since a few punctures will not cause a problem. Make sure that the liner of the spillway is tucked under the liner of the pond, as shown in figure 26.

Allowing for Inflow

In most cases, water will not be flowing into the pond, and you will just fill it using a garden hose. However, if the land surrounding the pond is higher than the edge, you can use it to provide water to top it up. If the pond is near the house, you can direct water from downspouts into the pond. In both cases, you need to figure out how to get the water flowing into the pond using an inflow, which is the reverse of a spillway. Use excess pond liner to direct water into the pond. Landscape the area so that the incoming water flows into a small creek that is lined and sloped to direct the water into the pond. The flowing water should not wash soil into the pond. An important difference between a spillway and an inflow is that the inflow liner should be laid on top of the pond liner, not under it for the spillway. This will ensure that water does not run under the pond liner.

Edging the Pond

With the pond now level and mostly filled with water, you will see pond liner all the way around the edge of the pond. The next step is to cover it as completely as possible. The pond liner is UV light resistant, but over time, sunlight will weaken it. Cover the liner very well so that no sunlight can reach it. This will also make the pond look more natural.

The trick to hiding the liner is to add the stones slowly, one at a time, positioning each one to fit tightly to the ones around it. It is a giant jigsaw puzzle where no stone seems to fit well. I like to pick up several stones and keep trying them until they fit well. Start with larger stones about the size of a cantaloupe, and then add smaller stones to fill any gaps. The pond will look more natural if you use a variety of different sized stones. When they are all in place, the pond will look very artificial with a ring of clean stones all the way around. Don't worry about this look. Most of the edge will eventually be covered with plants.

FIGURE 27
Beach area has been covered with smaller stones.

Adding the Finishing Touches

Several different materials can provide beach area. If the beach will be used by swimmers, use sand, which is easy to walk on, although it is so fine that it tends to run away to the deep part of the pond. A better option if you are not going to walk on the beach is to use small stones that are one to two inches in diameter. They look just as good, stay in place better, and animals can still use the beach. Add a few flatter stones showing just above the waterline to provide a drinking spot for birds.

The stones in the beach area are held in place by a ring of rocks on the inner shelf, similar to the planting shelves. Figure 24 shows the detail of these rocks.

FIGURE 28
Finished pond.

The spillway and inflow also need stones to cover the liner. At the edge of the pond, they should be large enough to hide the liner, but not so large that they prevent the movement of water. Place smaller stones farther away from the pond.

One of your last jobs is cut off the excess liner with a large pair of scissors. Never do the final cut until the pond is completely full of water and the edge has been leveled. Both of these tasks will change the amount of liner that you can cut off. Leave enough to overhang the edge of the pond by at least 6 inches (12 inches is safer) because soil settles and this excess amount will allow you to easily fix any problems around the edge. Then cover the remaining liner with either stones or soil.

Figure 28 shows a friend's pond that was used as a demonstration pond for this chapter. All of the rock work is complete. The overhanging dock has been added, and the area around the pond has been landscaped. Many more plants still need to be added. Right now it has that spanking clean new look, but it will look more and more natural each year.

Congratulations, the hard work is done. It is now time to add fish and plants, which are discussed in the next two chapters.

CHAPTER 6

Fish

As soon as you add the water, natural wildlife will find the pond. When I built my first pond, I had a frog in it the day after it filled. He must have been waiting for me to finish construction. This type of wildlife is all you really need. Fish do not have to be added, but they do provide a lot of extra enjoyment, and for some people, fish are the main reason for having a pond.

Fish can be detrimental to the pond. They like to eat the plants and the wildlife that comes to the pond. They will eat tadpoles and frog eggs, reducing the potential native populations. However, they also eat mosquito larvae, which is beneficial. Fish are a major contributor to nutrient overload that causes algae growth. Increasing the number of plants will overcome this problem.

Fish Care

Fish need three main things to stay healthy: oxygen, food, and low levels of ammonium. The best way to provide these is to maintain a small amount of fish. Fewer fish use less oxygen and produce less waste. The ammonium in the water comes from fish waste; less ammonium keeps fish healthier.

Food is not really a problem in a natural pond. Unless you are raising game fish, you don't need to feed the fish at all. Let them find their own food. My goldfish never get fed. They grow quickly and find lots of food. If insect populations are low, they will eat more algae.

It is not the number of fish but their weight that counts, although most people talk in terms of fish length because it is easier to measure. A ten-inch fish is about equal to ten one-inch fish. Fish grow, so you need to consider their adult size. Some types will breed in the pond, and you should allow extra room for the babies.

How many fish can you add? As a general rule, keep your fish load under one inch of adult fish, not including the tail, for every one square foot of surface area. Less is always better. Adding more fish will increase the strain on plants to keep the water clean. In the natural pond, it is essential to balance the amount of fish with the number of plants.

If you have just filled the pond, don't rush to add the fish. Give the water a week to settle and allow any chlorine to dissipate into the air. This also gives insects time to find the pond so the fish have something to eat. When you bring the fish home, float the bag in the pond for about 30 minutes to let the temperature inside the bag reach that of the pond. Then release the fish.

Some people recommend adding salt or other tonics to a new pond, especially for koi. Salt can help fish fight disease, and it helps fish swim easier in the higher-density water. Unfortunately, salt is not good for plants. Salt and tonics are not needed in a natural pond. Remove any sick fish and treat them in a separate container.

Many articles talk about adding bacteria to "charge" the pond, claiming that they are needed to maintain low ammonium levels. It is true that bacteria do this, but it is not true that you need to add them. They start colonizing the pond even before you finish building it. The rocks, plants, and even your dirty hands have added billions of bacteria. Don't add more.

The following sections describe the more common fish in man-made ponds, and you do not have to select just one type. Except for the mosquito fish, which will become food for the larger fish, you can include several types. Overwintering fish will be discussed in more detail in the chapter on pond maintenance.

Hobby Fish

Goldfish

Goldfish, an excellent choice for most backyard ponds, are highly recommended if you have never had fish before. They are inexpensive, will find their own food, and can overwinter outside in most regions. They are easy to maintain, will breed in small ponds, and provide a lot of enjoyment.

You can buy fancy goldfish for your pond, but most people buy feeder fish, one- to two-inch fish sold, by the dozen at a low price, at pet stores as food for larger fish. The problem with feeder fish is they are not all very healthy, and in my experience, about 30 percent will die in a day or two. The rest will grow and prosper in the pond, so it is still a good deal, and you save 70 percent from being eaten.

Goldfish need to be about four inches long before they will breed. They might breed in the first year, more likely in the second spring. After a while, you may have too many fish, but a visit from the local heron or raccoon will solve the problem. If they don't eat enough fish, you might need to remove some so that they don't produce too much fish waste.

In most regions, goldfish will overwinter, provided the pond is deep enough not to freeze solid. Most people just leave them in the pond to fend for themselves over winter.

There are also many fancy goldfish for you to try. Comets have straight, darting bodies of red-gold. Fantails with their flowing fancy tails move gracefully through the water. The black Chinese Moor has telescopic eyes.

Koi

Koi are very popular and make good fish for medium- and large-sized ponds. They are available in a magnificent variety of colors and patterns, including metallic and multicolored. They can be trained to eat out of your hand and to come when you call them.

These fish grow much larger than goldfish, and many people end up with too much fish for the size of their pond. Koi grow to two feet long, and as adults, they each require 100 square feet of surface area. Each fish should have at least 300 gallons of water. They also require cleaner water and higher oxygen levels than goldfish, which makes them a bit harder to keep. The key is to keep fish levels low.

If you are considering koi, you probably need to decide if your interest in a natural pond is because you want the pond or because you want to keep koi. The two are not perfect partners although they can co-exist. The problem is that koi like to eat plants, and they disturb roots just for the fun of it. They also produce a lot of fish waste, in part because koi owners like to baby their fish and feed them a lot.

A pond with koi that continually disturb the plants will end up with algae problems. One solution is to physically separate the plants from the koi by making the inner edge of the planting shelves higher so that the fish can't enter the area where plants grow. It will still look like one pond, but underwater it will have several distinct sections.

In colder regions, most koi are taken inside for the winter. If they are left outside, the pond should be at least four feet deep; many koi owners prefer five feet.

Another issue with koi in natural ponds is that herons like to come for a meal. Since koi can be expensive, most owners are not too happy when this happens. Some will even keep their ponds covered with netting all of the time. This works but does not look very natural.

You can certainly keep koi in your natural pond, but they are probably not the best choice.

Mosquito Fish

Mosquito fish, small guppy-like fish in the genus *Gambusia*, are native to North and Central America. They grow up to two inches long and consume large quantities of insect larvae as well as algae. They are mostly silver or light brown and breed easily in small ponds. They are not as interesting to look at as goldfish or koi, but they do a great job keeping the pond free of mosquitoes.

There are several different species of mosquito fish. If you live in colder climates, get some local varieties that are much more tolerant of cold than southern species. Northern mosquito fish can overwinter in the north; southern varieties will not. They can be difficult to catch, so it is best to leave them in the pond over winter.

Unlike koi and goldfish, males and females are easy to differentiate. The males are smaller, thinner, and have a pointed anal fin, like that of a guppy. Females have a dark pregnancy patch on the lower portion of the body.

Golden Orfe

The golden orfe (*Leuciscus idus*) is native to Europe, where it inhabits lakes and slow-moving streams. They are very active, orange or golden, and spend much of their time at the surface of the water. Unless kept in a school of at least six, they tend to be shy.

Because adults are almost two feet long, they need to have a larger pond. A school of six fish make a spectacular display. They are not easy to breed, which can be a good thing since too many baby fish can be a problem. They seem to only breed when they get older.

Like koi, orfes require higher levels of oxygen. This is not a problem in a large pond in summer but may be in winter. They can overwinter in ponds that do not freeze solid, but such ponds can have oxygen levels that are too low. For this reason, it might be best to bring the fish inside in zones 6 and lower. To better understand hardiness zones, consult the link provided in the References section.

Game Fish

Game fish are selected based on the temperature of the water, size of pond, and availability of breeding areas. Each type has a preferred habitat for breeding, and if this is important, make sure the pond is designed for your chosen fish.

Small ponds will only accommodate one type of fish. Larger ponds, over an acre in size, can accommodate two or even three. These also provide more variety in habitats and temperature ranges.

Fish have a preferred range of temperature, and if it gets too high, they will get sick and die. Cold water fish need water that never goes over 70°F. Cool water fish can have temperatures go above 70°F, but they should rarely reach 80°F. Warm water fish live comfortably in summer temperatures up to 90°F.

Stock the pond with fish from a breeder to reduce the chance of introducing a disease into your pond. In some areas, it is illegal to stock a pond with captured fish. Avoid adding the following fish: crappie, bullhead, yellow perch, pumpkinseed, carp, sucker, flathead catfish, blue catfish, and green sunfish.

Largemouth Bass

The largemouth or black bass is a primary sport fish. Growth rates vary depending on pond conditions, density, and genetics. They can reach ten inches by their third year. Their diet consists of insects when they are small and changes to fish as adults. These warm water fish spawn in spring, at 60°F, in the shallow margins of the pond.

Bluegill

The bluegill is considered a secondary sport fish and may be feeders for other types of fish. They can grow up to six inches in their first year in optimal conditions, maturing at eight inches in their second or third year. This warm water fish spawns in shallow water at about 75°F and prefers to eat insects.

Redear Sunfish

The redear is a secondary sport fish with growth rates and spawning habits similar to the bluegill except that they produce fewer young. These cool water fish eat insects and snails at the bottom of the pond and are considered a biological control for a snail parasite that causes swimmers itch in humans.

Channel Catfish

The channel catfish, prized for their eating quality, thrives in small ponds. They spawn once temperatures reach 72°F and continue spawning for the summer. These warm water fish get along with other types and are routinely used as a secondary fish. They eat just about anything, including crayfish, insects, and small fish.

Flathead Minnow

This minnow is used as a forage fish for the largemouth bass and reaches a length of four inches. They have warm water spawning habits and may spawn in a pond.

Rainbow Trout

This cold water fish is an excellent choice, provided the temperature never goes above 70°F. They grow most rapidly between 50° and 65°F. Usually stocked at six-inch fingerlings, they can weigh eight ounces at the end of the first year. Like channel catfish, they readily take pelletized food and can be maintained in small ponds. Rainbows rarely reproduce in recreational ponds and must be restocked.

CHAPTER 7

Plants

Plants are absolutely critical for making your natural pond work. They serve three roles:

- Aesthetically, they make the pond look natural.
- They remove excess nutrients.
- They increase oxygen levels.

The most vital of these is the second one: removing nutrients. Fish, frogs, and insects all add waste material to the water. Plant debris landing on the water adds more organic material, and the microbes you can't see are dying and adding to the organic load. All of this will be converted into nutrients over time, resulting in an accumulation of things like nitrogen, phosphorus, and potassium.

As nutrient levels rise, algae will start to grow. To control algae, the pond needs enough plants to absorb all of the excess nutrients before the algae can use them. How many plants are needed to do this job? That is a difficult question to answer since there are just too many variables to consider. From experience, I have found that if one-third to one-half of the pond's surface area is filled with established plants, the pond will be algae-free. This will be augmented with some floating water lilies.

Due to limited space, this book will only describe plants that grow in water. The area around the pond can include any plants that you might normally grow in your garden.

Some garden plants like to grow wet, and many sources suggest planting them near a stream or pond. That is true provided these water features are native or if they are built without a liner. A pond built with a liner does not have an edge that stays wet since the liner prevents the water from seeping into the soil around the pond. Moisture-loving plants won't do much better beside a lined pond than anywhere else in the garden.

Planting

The standard way to add plants to a pond is to set them in pots containing soil. There are two problems with this approach. First, the plants soon outgrow their pots, and then you need to divide and replant them. This is just too much work. The second problem is the soil. It contains nutrients. In the garden, plants use the nutrients in the soil to grow, but in a natural pond, the plants should be using the nutrients in the water, not nutrients from soil. Adding soil to a pond just increases its nutrient level, something we are trying to avoid. For a natural pond, the rule is simple: don't use soil.

All a plant really needs is a way to anchor itself to the bottom of the pond, and many don't even need that. Instead of soil to hold them down, the natural pond system uses small stones. Planting is very simple. Place them where you want them on the planting shelf and put a larger rock on the roots to hold them in place. In no time at all, the roots will attach themselves to the smaller rocks in the planting shelf. In a month or so, you can remove the larger rock or leave it in place. The plants don't care.

This system works so well that, after two years, when you want to thin out your plants, you might actually have a problem lifting them out. The root mass becomes huge. But that is a good problem to have. All of these roots are absorbing nutrients from the water.

Water plants can be added in any season, since the roots are in water and there is no fear of them drying out.

Fertilizing

Every other pond book will tell you to fertilize your plants, but in the natural pond, you want to reduce nutrients not increase them. Never fertilize a plant in the pond.

What happens if a plant can't get enough nutrients? It slows down or even stops growing for a while. Some older leaves might go yellow as nutrients are moved from them to newer leaves. That won't kill the plant. A lack of nutrients in the water is rarely a problem. If plants are really struggling and you have no algae problems, you can try adding a bit of fertilizer to the pond, but it is probably better to just wait until nature takes over and adds nutrients for you.

Starting Small

Gardens normally develop with time. At the beginning of a new garden, all you have is bare soil. You then add a few small plants or trees, and things look very bare. It takes several years to have plants establish themselves and grow into larger clumps. After a few years, the garden starts to look full and mature.

Pond gardens are no different. Most people start by buying a few plants and adding them to the pond. It will look bare at first. Over time the plants will grow and fill in. The problem with this approach is that a few plants might not use enough nutrients to keep algae at bay. It is not uncommon for new ponds to have algae problems for the first year or two. As the plants fill in and get larger, the algae problem starts to disappear all on its own.

When I started my main pond, I added very few plants, and by mid-summer, the water was green with planktonic algae. I even had some string algae in the beach area. By year three, there was very little algae, and after that, plants kept things in control.

Adding plants slowly makes financial sense, but you can decide to add lots of plants right away and eliminate the algae problem from day one.

Too Many Plants

It comes as no surprise that plants grow, and they seem to grow faster in water than on land. In no time at all, your plants will start to get crowded. You then need to make a decision. Will you leave the plants alone and let them fight it out to see who survives? Or will you keep each type of plant under control? Either option works regarding the health of the pond, but aesthetically it might be best to control plants a bit. A pond looks much better with several different kinds of plants than just one type.

To control the plants, you will need to pull some out periodically and get rid of them. This will improve air circulation between the plants, help reduce plant diseases, and make room for more growth, which keeps taking nutrients out of the water. When you are removing a plant, take out the old part and leave the young growing tips. The resulting plants will thrive and look better.

Plant Pests and Diseases

Water plants have very few pests and diseases. Some insect pests might affect the appearance of plants but they rarely kill a plant. Roots can get a bacterial rot, but even that is rare. Fish and turtles may nibble on plants. It is best to remove dead or dying leaves and any diseased plants.

A lot of pond advice suggests that plants need to be fed regularly to keep them healthy, but this is not required in a natural pond. The natural microbes will solve the problem for you. I'll discuss plant cleanup in more detail in the maintenance chapter.

Undesirable Pond Plants

Some pond plants grow too easily, and they should not be added to a new pond. For example, duckweed, a small plant that floats, looks good, uses lots of nutrients, and reduces the amount of light reaching the pond surface. This all sounds great, but once you have duckweed in your pond, you can't get rid of it. Every little piece will start to grow again, quickly. Try to keep it out of your pond if possible. If it does invade your pond, you will need to scoop it out once or twice a season and put it on your garden as a free mulch.

Many pond books recommend including submersible plants. Their main purpose is to add oxygen to the water, which they do fairly well, but they also die easily. I have never used them, and I see no reason for adding them to the pond.

Some aquatic plants have become invasive in native wetlands, and these should not be used. Their invasiveness depends on your climate. Plants that grow well in warm zones may not live through the winter in colder zones. For example, water lettuce is invading natural wetlands in warmer regions, but it will not overwinter in zone 5. In cold climates, it is not invasive.

Each state or country will have its own list of invasive aquatics, and you should review them before buying plants. The following are some of the more common invasive water plants.

- Alligator weed, *Alternanthera philoxeroides*
- Brazilian waterweed, *Egeria densa*
- Caulerpa, Mediterranean clone, *Caulerpa taxiflia*
- Chameleon plant, *Houttuynia cordata*
- Common reed, *Phragmites australis*
- Curly pondweed, *Potamogeton crispus*
- Didymo, *Didymosphenia geminata*
- Eurasian watermilfoil, *Myriophyllum spicatum*
- European frogbit, *Hydrocharis morsus-ranae*
- Flowering rush, *Butomus umbellatus*
- Giant reed, *Arundo donax*
- Giant salvinia, *Salvinia molesta*
- Horsetail, *Equisetum* sp.
- Hydrilla, *Hydrilla verticillata*
- Knotweed, *Fallopia japonica*
- Melaleuca, *Melaleuca quinquenervia*
- Purple loosestrife, *Lythrum salicaria*
- Reed canary grass, *Phalaris arundinacea*
- Water chestnut, *Trapa natans*
- Water hyacinth, *Eichhornia crassipes*
- Water lettuce, *Pistia stratiote*
- Water spinach, *Ipomoea aquatica*
- Yellow flag iris, *Iris pseudacorus*

Selection of Water Plants

Name	Zone Light	Plant Height Planting Depth	Flowering time Flower color	Description
Acorus calamus Sweet flag	4–11 Sun to shade	4 ft 6 in	Summer Yellow	Slow grower, looks like iris, see description below
Alisma lanceolatum Water plantain	3–11 Sun to part shade	1 ft 6 in	Summer to fall White	Flowers are large misty heads with lots of small flowers
Aponogeton distachyos Water hawthorn	5–11 Sun to part shade	Surface 6 in–4 ft	Summer White	Goes dormant in warm weather
Calla palustris Bog arum	2–6 Sun	6 in 6 in	Spring White	Red seed heads in fall, likes acidic water
Caltha palustris Marsh marigold	3–7 Sun to shade	1 ft 6 in	Spring Yellow	See description below
Canna spp. Cannas	8–11 Sun	2–9 ft 6–12 in	Summer to fall Various	Dramatic plants, flowers first year from seed
Colocasia spp. Elephant ears, taro	9–11 Sun	2–6 ft 6 in	No flower	Bold, large leaves in greens and dark purple
Cyperus alternifolius Umbrella grass	7–11 Sun to part shade	4–6 ft 6 in	No flower	Tall stately plant, oriental look, see description below
Eichhornia crassipes Water hyacinth	9–11 Sun	1 ft Floating	Summer Lavender	Grow as annual only in colder areas where it cannot escape into the wild
Hottonia palustris Featherfoil, water violet	6–11 Sun to part shade	6 in 1 ft	Summer White	Roots and then floats out into the water
Iris spp. Iris	4–10 Sun	1–3 ft 6 in	Summer Various	See description below
Juncus effusus Common rush	3–11 Sun to part shade	6 in 2–3 ft	No flower	Does best if water level is low in summer
Juncus effusus 'Spiralis' Corkscrew rush	3–11 Sun to part shade	6 in 2–3 ft	No flower	Unusual twisted stems
Nelumbo spp. Lotus	5–11 Sun	2–4 ft 2–3 ft	Summer to fall Various	Aggressive grower
Nymphaea spp. Small water lilies	9–11 Sun	Surface 1 ft	Summer to fall Various	See description below
Nymphaea spp. Large water lilies	9–11 Sun	Surface 2–3 ft	Summer to fall Various	See description below
Pistia stratiotes Water lettuce	9–11 Part shade to shade	6 in Floating	No flower	Grow as annual only in colder areas where it cannot escape into the wild
Pontederia cordata Blue pickerel weed	3–10 Sun to part shade	2–4 ft 6 in	Summer to fall Blue or white	Heart-shaped leaves, see description below
Sagittaria latifolia Arrowhead	3–11 Sun to part shade	1 ft 6 in	Summer White	Can be aggressive, see description below

Name	Zone Light	Plant Height Planting Depth	Flowering time Flower color	Description
Saururus cernuus Lizard's tail	5–11 Sun to part shade	2 ft 6 in	Summer White	Rhizomes do not tolerate being frozen
Symplocarpus foetidus Skunk cabbage	3–9 Part shade	1 ft 3 in	Spring Speckled red	Grown mostly for the large leaves
Thalia dealbata Thalia	6–11 Sun to part shade	2–6 ft 6 in	Summer Purple	Distinctive upright leaves
Typha spp. Cattail	3–11 Sun to part shade	2–9 ft 1 ft	Summer Green	Distinctive seed heads
Zizania aquatica Wild rice	5–11 Sun	3–7 ft 1–2 ft	Summer Green	Distinct large flower heads

Workhorse Water Plants

Many plants can grow in water, but most owners find it beneficial to include several of the following workhorse plants. They are all easy to get, are long-lived, and grow very well in water. This list also includes some of the most attractive flowering plants. Once you have some of these established, have fun and try some of the more obscure plants.

Iris

There are many different species of iris, and when most people hear the name, they think of the very colorful German bearded iris, which does not grow well in water. Many other types of iris will grow as marginal plants in shallow water. Most have vertical grass-like leaves that look very natural both beside and in the water. Irises also have some of the most spectacular flowers you will find in a pond.

Most iris form a fleshy root called a tuber. New leaves are produced at the tip of the tuber, and the back of it slowly dies away over several years. You can easily divide the plants by simply snapping the tuber into pieces, making sure that each has a growing eye on it. Plant the tubers two inches below the surface of the water and place a larger stone on them to hold them in place. If the tuber ends up above the waterline in late summer, they will be fine as long as the roots are submerged.

FIGURE 29
Iris ensata,
Japanese iris.

The following iris species are worth adding to your pond. They are available in many colors and bloom at different times of the year. Select a variety so you always have something in flower.

- *Iris siberica* (Siberian iris): this iris is easy to grow both in normal soil and in very wet soil, but it does not like to be submerged. It is best in a rain garden or bog garden. Ideal for zones 4 to 8.
- *Iris ensata* (Japanese iris): this has some of the most spectacular flowers. It grows in moist soil as well as very shallow water. It does not like to grow in water that freezes solid, but does fine in my zone 5 pond. Suitable for zones 3 to 9.
- *Iris laevigata* (Japanese water iris): this is easy to grow in zones 4 to 9 and is available with variegated leaves. This is a true water iris and can be grown in six inches of water.
- *Iris* ser. *Hexagonae* (Louisiana iris): this grows taller than other iris and has large flowers. These marsh plants like to grow with their tubers under water, even up to a foot deep. Grows in zones 5 to 10.

Water Lilies

Nymphaea species are extremely valuable to the pond. They not only look great and flower well, but the floating leaves provide shade, eliminating the light needed by algae. They also provide a hiding place for fish and other water creatures. Water lilies should cover half of the open water space to help maintain a balanced ecosystem. They do best in quiet water, so keep them away from fountains and waterfalls.

Water lilies can grow into large plants. The tubers elongate and divide each year, forming larger and larger clumps. Larger varieties will eventually take over the whole pond. They like lots of sun to bloom well, and if they are happy, they will bloom most of the summer and fall. In warm regions, they can bloom all year long.

FIGURE 30
A large, hardy water lily.

Water lilies are available in two major categories, hardy and tropical. The hardy water lilies will grow well and overwinter in cold climates. The tropicals can also be grown in cold climates, but they need to be brought inside for the winter since they can't take frost. The tropical plants are more trouble for gardeners in cold climates, but their flowers are larger and the colors are more luminescent. Many gardeners think the extra effort is worth it.

The plants themselves are available in various sizes. Small-leafed plants normally have smaller flowers and grow more slowly. Large-leafed ones have the largest flowers and grow faster. Medium-sized ones have characteristics halfway between the small and large. Match the size of plant to the size of pond. Large lilies should be given at least 100 square feet of open water space. The small ones will get lost in a big pond and are more suitable to small ponds and other small water features, including water tubs. These plants are quite adaptable to different water depths, but the large ones prefer being two to three feet deep and the small ones like to be 6 to 12 inches deep. If they are a bit too deep, it takes them longer to get leaves to the surface of the water in spring, but they will get there. Such plants will, over time, grow tubers higher up in the water to a level where they like to live.

Water lilies are heavy feeders, and many people feed them regularly, but that is not necessary. In a natural pond, the plants need to use the nutrients in the pond and not added fertilizer. In theory you could just lay the tubers on the bottom of the pond and they will grow. The problem is that the tubers float. Therefore it is better to put them into a pot along with some stones to hold them under water. Don't use any soil or fertilizer. In a year or two, they will outgrow the pot, and you can just let them do their own thing at the bottom of the pond.

When you add a new water lily to the pond, place it on a shallow shelf for a while until leaves grow. Once it is established, lower it to its final depth. Water lilies naturally replace leaves every few weeks; those that are now too low will simply be replaced with leaves that have a longer petiole.

Hardy Water Lilies

Hardy water lilies grow in zones 4 to 11, and the flowers come in a variety of colors and shapes. Some even change their color as they age. Most varieties have green leaves, but some have a nice mottled color as well. For cold climate gardeners, these lilies bloom earlier in the year than tropicals, since they will bloom in colder water (60°F). These easy-care plants have no problem with a winter freeze, provided that the tubers are below the ice. In warmer climates, they can flower all year long.

Hardies, as they are known, will open their flowers in the morning and stay open all day. Late in the day and on cloudy days, they will close. Each flower lasts three to five days, with new ones continually being formed. An established plant will have several flowers open at any given time.

The plants can be left alone to continue growing until they get too big. At some point, you will have to get into the pond and remove the whole clump. If you don't do this every five years, the clump may get too big to remove. By this time, the plant will have made many side branches on the tuber, and you will be able to break or cut off any number of young growths. The rest can be given to friends.

Tropical Water Lilies

Tropical water lilies normally grow in zones 9 to 11, but they can be grown in colder zones as an annual. At the end of the season, bring them into the house over the winter and then return them in spring.

These lilies are available as day-blooming or night-blooming plants. Night bloomers, which tend to be more fragrant, will open their flowers at dusk and keep them open until about 10:00 AM the following day, a couple of hours longer on cloudy days. Day bloomers open at about 9:00 AM and close at 5:00 PM. People who work never see their day bloomers open except on weekends. Some varieties of day bloomers do stay open until late evening. All of these times are approximate and will change with climate, location, and variety.

The challenge with tropical water lilies in cold climates is overwintering them. They need to be kept at a minimum of 45°F. The best way to do this is to remove the plant from the pond in fall and cut off all leaves and flowers. You will be left with round tubers the size of a golf ball or even smaller. Pack these in a glass jar along with some damp peat moss and store at 45°F to 50°F for the winter. In spring take out the tubers and warm them up so that they start to grow. Return them to the pond once the temperature stays above 70°F.

Marsh Marigold

Caltha palustris, also known as marsh marigold, is a great addition to shallow water areas. They are easy to grow and flower in late April and May before most other water plants bloom. They multiply easily and quickly fill whatever space is allotted to them.

Marsh marigolds usually have single yellow flowers, but a white form, called alba, is also available. *Caltha palustris* 'Flore pleno' is a yellow double-flowered form. They prefer lots of sun but flower quite well in a shady spot, which is one reason for their popularity. At 12 inches tall, they can be used to fill small areas around the pond or under larger plants.

FIGURE 31
Caltha palustris,
marsh marigold.

These plants will grow well in zones 3 to 7, but in warmer climates they might die back in the heat of summer. Plant in small stones that stay moist without standing water; they will also do well in six inches of water. They require no regular maintenance and can survive winter freezing in ice.

The leaves of marsh marigold are edible if cooked properly. If they are not cooked well enough, the toxin protoanemonin will cause burning in the throat, vomiting, and bloody diarrhea. Think twice about eating it unless you know what you are doing.

FIGURE 32
Typha species, cattails.

Cattail

The cattail is represented by several species of the genus *Typha*. In North America, *T. latifolia*, the broad-leaved cattail, and *T. angustifolia*, the narrow-leaved cattail, are natives. These wetland plants can grow from three to ten feet tall. They are one of the most commonly seen plants in marshy wetlands, and because of this, they add a very natural look to your pond. *Typha minima* is a dwarf cattail that grows to three feet tall and may be more suitable for smaller ponds.

The problem with cattails is that they are aggressive. These very strong growers will out-compete most other plants. Without some management, they will soon fill a large part of a shallow pond. The natural pond design discussed in this book will restrict their growth to the planting shelves, but within a shelf, they can take over. In a shallow earth bottom pond, it will be more difficult to control their growth.

I grow both taller species of cattail in my pond, and neither was planted. Within a few months of filling the pond, the first ones started growing from seeds blown in from somewhere.

I do have to remove excess plants from time to time, but they are such great plants that I will keep them.

The narrow long leaves sway gently in the wind, and dragonflies love to sit on them. In mid- to late summer, they produce the characteristic brown cattail, which is a very unusual seed head. It remains on the plant most of the winter and falls apart into fuzzy seeds in early spring.

The plants grow best in warm water that is less than two feet deep. Once they are well established, the tubers can float out over the water and slowly expand as a floating raft over deeper water.

Cattails in larger ponds provide nesting habitat for birds like the red-winged blackbird and various kinds of ducks. They are great at preventing erosion of dams and pond banks. Since these vigorous growers remove a lot of nutrients, they are an excellent way to keep the water clean and algae free. If all of this growth is allowed to drop back into the pond at the end of the season, then the nutrients will just accumulate over time. For this reason, you should remove the old plant growth in fall or winter. This is easily done if your pond freezes over.

FIGURE 33
Acorus calamus, sweet flag or scented rush.

Sweet Flag

Acorus calamus is also known as sweet flag or scented rush. The "sweet" in the name comes from the fragrance given off when the leaves or rhizomes are broken or bruised. It is a good addition to a bog or pond because it is easy to grow and the white in the variegated leaves adds extra interest all summer long.

Sweet flag will grow to about two and one-half feet and will spread slowly. The green flowers are formed in a weird clump called a spadix. It is unusual but not particularly ornamental. It can grow in sun or part shade, in moist soil or standing in water. Some shade is appreciated in very hot climates. It is very adaptable in zones 4 to 11.

It is native to Europe but has naturalized in many areas in the northeastern United States. The plant that is normally sold is a triploid, so it does not make seeds. This helps control its spread in the wild and in your garden.

The variegated form of sweet flag has a creamy-white strip beside a green strip and grows about two feet tall. It is more popular but does grow slower than the green form.

The plant is easy to propagate by splitting the rhizome, similar to an iris. It goes fully dormant in winter and has no problem being frozen in ice.

Arrowhead

Sagittaria latifolia, the arrowhead plant, provides unique arrow-shaped leaves as well as dainty white flowers. It is easy to grow in shallow water and does best in full sun where it flowers well but can also grow in part shade. The flowers appear above the leaves that can reach up to three feet above the water.

FIGURE 34
Sagittaria latifolia, arrowhead.

This North American native should be planted in 6 to 12 inches of water. It grows fine in zones 4 to 10 where it does not need special winter protection.

Arrowhead is also called duck potato and wapato, which refer to the starchy golf-ball-sized tubers it forms at the end of rhizome. These can break off and float on top of the water. They can be boiled or baked and eaten like a potato. Waterfowl also like to eat then, hence the name duck potato.

Pickerel Weed

Pickerel weed (*Pontedaria cordata*) is native to North America where it covers a wide range from Nova Scotia to Florida, and west to Texas. Hardy in zones 3 to 10, it will grow in almost any condition, provided its roots are in water. It needs no special winter care, and full sun provides the best flowering.

Flowers develop in late summer as a three- to six-inch flower cluster that is very showy. A white flowering form exists, but most people prefer the blue one. Flowers open from the bottom of the spike to the top, providing a long display. The nectar attracts many insects, including bees and butterflies.

The plant grows to two to four feet and can be planted in six inches of water. It spreads rapidly, using rhizomes to form dense colonies that are great for cleaning nutrients out of water. It is easily divided by breaking the rhizomes into pieces, with each containing at least one growing eye.

The seeds, which can be eaten raw right from the plant or dried and stored for future use, make a good addition to granola cereal.

FIGURE 35
Pontedaria cordata,
pickerel weed.

InAweofGod'sCreation, under creative common license, photo was modified

Umbrella Palm

The umbrella palm is related to papyrus and forms a very unusual stem with leaves at the top in the shape of an umbrella. This plant gives the pond a very tropical look. It will grow in sun or part shade and has inconspicuous green flowers. As it grows, it forms a tight bunch that does not spread. Plant at two to six inches deep. Smaller varieties prefer less water; plant larger ones deeper. Figure 7 shows the umbrella plant growing in a pond.

The name for this species and some varieties is very mixed up in the marketplace, and it is likely that any plant you buy is mislabeled. Look at the size of the plant you buy instead of trying to sort out the right name.

The following varieties are available.

Credit: Forest and Kim Starr, under creative common license, photo was modified.

FIGURE 36
Cyperus species, umbrella palm.

- *Cyperus alternifolius* 'Gracilis': the dwarf umbrella palm, grows to two feet.
- *Cyperus alternifolius* 'Variegatus': the variegated dwarf umbrella palm, grows to two feet and has variegated stems and leaves. If stems grow that are all green, cut them off or they will take over the plant.
- *Cyperus involucratus*: the giant or large umbrella palm, grows to five feet.

None of the umbrella palms can overwinter in cold weather. Take the plants inside in fall and grow them as house plants in normal soil until spring, when you can return them to the pond. Alternatively, cut off all foliage and store in a cool dark place, like a fruit cellar or a garage, that does not freeze. In spring warm up the plant and return it to the pond.

CHAPTER 8

Maintenance and Troubleshooting

The great thing about a natural pond is that regular maintenance is almost nonexistent. Top up the pond when it needs water. Add a bubbler in winter if you have fish. Spend an hour a year taking out some organic matter. Sit and enjoy the pond.

If you read other pond instructional books or search the internet, you'll find all kinds of things you need to do to keep a pond healthy. That advice might be right for the pond design they use, but it is not applicable for the natural pond design described in this book. You can skip most of that advice.

Don't Do These Things

This section describes routine maintenance tasks for other pond systems that are not required for natural ponds. They are included with explanations for why you don't have to do them.

Check pH

Because fish and plants have a preferred range of pH that they need in order to live, it makes sense to check that its level is right. The problem is, what do you do if it is wrong? As different biological processes become more dominant, pH fluctuates. Warm days will have a different pH than cold days. Early in the season will be different from late in the season. How often are you going to try to control this?

The only way to control pH is to use chemicals. Once you start adding chemicals to control pH, you will need to continually check it and keep adding chemicals—a never-ending process. Each time it rains or you add more water, you need to check the pH and adjust it. I strongly believe that continually changing the pH level is worse for life in the pond than leaving it alone.

It is very unlikely that your drinking water has such an extreme pH that it will not support fish and plants. It may not be ideal, but it will be satisfactory. If you drink the water, the fish and plants will be fine.

Adding Bacteria

Regular pond care requires that you add bacteria to keep the filters charged. In spring you add them to get the filters going. In fall you are supposed to add special bacteria for cold weather. If the pump is turned off for a while, the bacteria in the filter die and you need to add more when you restart it. Many people add bacteria twice a week—just to be sure.

Some of this might be beneficial if you have a complex filter system or have too many fish. Otherwise, adding bacteria makes no sense. They find the pond on their own, and they don't die off that quickly. If environmental conditions turn against them, they go into a type of hibernation until the conditions are favorable again. A natural pond is full of many different types of bacteria. Some grow better in warm weather and some in cold weather. You don't need to add more.

Measure Ammonium

Fish waste contains a lot of ammonium (same as ammonia). If the levels get too high, the fish can die. So some pond owners are constantly checking to make sure they are safe. If levels get too high, they add a handful of bacteria to solve the problem.

The alternative is to keep fish levels lower and don't add food, so you never have this problem. High ammonium levels are the result of too much fish poop. If you control the poop levels, you will not have ammonium problems.

Ammonium is also converted to nitrite and nitrate by bacteria (see figure 2). A natural pond design has plenty of microbes to take care of any ammonium produced by fish. It does not need to be checked.

Measure Oxygen Levels

Fish breathe oxygen, and if the levels get too low, they can suffocate. This will not happen in a pond with a normal number of fish, but some people cram a lot of fish into a small pond for a better display. They artificially create a situation where it is very easy to run out of oxygen. In this case, you need to keep monitoring the oxygen levels. If they get low, you turn on auxiliary pumps and fountains to increase the gas exchange between water and air. An alternate solution is to have fewer fish.

Cleaning the Pond

After a few months or a year, all of the surfaces in the pond become covered in slime. To the uninformed, this is a bad thing, and they want to clean it out. Many maintenance schedules call for you to empty the pond water once a year in order to scrub the sides of the liner and remove the slime. Once the pond is crystal clear, you refill it and dump in some purchased bacteria.

What these people don't understand is that the slime layer is made up of microbes, including bacteria. They need to add bacteria to the water because the cleaning process just removed them all. This makes no sense. Just leave the beneficial slime in place and go have a beer.

Natural ponds do not need to be cleaned on a regular basis. Instead, you do everything you can to grow as much slime as possible. In our ponds, the slime is our natural water filter and pond cleaner. My pond is almost ten years old and has never been cleaned. The water is crystal clear.

Reducing Algae

Algae growth is a big problem with pond owners since they don't like the look of it. The simple solution is to add algaecides that will kill the growth. This works—to a certain point. The dead then settle on the bottom and start to decompose, which releases nutrients into the water that feeds more algae growth. No problem, add more chemicals.

In these types of ponds, the algae problem is never solved. It recurs several times a summer, year after year. A bigger pump and better filtration system might help. In a natural pond, you will get some algae especially in the first couple of years while the plants are getting settled. The first summer after putting in my pond, the water was a solid pea green color due to algae. I lived with it. It did not harm any life-forms in the pond and gave the fish lots to eat. As plants got established, the algae stopped growing. Three years after putting in the pond, it had almost no algae, and it has been clear ever since. If your algae problem persists, add more plants or reduce the number of fish. Algae will not grow without sun and nutrients.

Adding Water

Water will evaporate from your pond, and the level will go down. How fast does this happen? It depends on many things. Warmer days evaporate water faster than cold days, so the drop in level is very much dependent on climate and time of year. Plants give off water as they photosynthesize. More plants will evaporate more water. The amount of daily precipitation has a big effect on water levels as does any source of inflow.

Keep in mind that spring and fall rains usually top up ponds that then dry down during the summer. If you add water, don't do it before the spring rains are finished, or you might add too much.

The design of the natural pond is such that the pond can lose several inches of water without any problem. It still looks natural at lower water levels. Once the roots of your plants get too exposed, you could add some more water. My zone 5 pond usually gets topped up once in late summer, and I don't add too much water because we get fall rains. It has no natural sources of water except for rain and snow.

If your tap water is highly chlorinated, consider adding smaller amounts so that chlorine can evaporate. Too much is harmful to plants and animals. Spraying the water in a mist from the end of a hose will also help dissipate chlorine.

Although all water contains some salts, hard water can contain a lot. As water evaporates, the salts are left behind. This is why your kettle gets a white hard layer in the bottom—these are the salts left behind after water boils off. The same thing happens in a pond. Over time the amount of salt in the pond increases as more and more water evaporates. These salts are mostly made up of calcium and magnesium, which plants use to grow but only small amounts are needed. If you have hard water, partially empty the pond every few years and replace it with fresh water. The frequency of doing this depends on the hardness of your water. Because mine is fairly hard, I replace half every five years. You could get more scientific than this and measure the conductivity of your water, but it is not really necessary, since calcium and magnesium are not very toxic to plants or animals.

Removing Organics

Organic matter in the pond comes from falling leaves, dead material from pond plants, and even dead microbes. This all collects at the bottom. You will find that the water in your pond is quite clear and has no real odor. If you disturb the muck at the bottom, the water will get cloudy and stink like rotten eggs. The smell is due to the anaerobic decomposition taking place in the bottom of the pond.

A natural pond can handle a certain amount of organic muck. As it accumulates, it is decomposed, and the nutrients produced are absorbed by growing plants. It is, however, a good idea to limit the amount of organic material collecting in the pond. Having less muck is always a good thing.

If you have a lot of muck, remove it once or twice a year. Fall is a good time so that you can also remove the newly fallen leaves. Just use a pond net and take out most of the stuff—you are not trying to get every last bit. The muck you remove makes excellent mulch for the garden. In eight years, I have never cleaned out my larger pond, but I do clean out the smaller one annually. It has fewer plants so it can't handle as many nutrients, and it collects a lot of leaves from surrounding trees.

What about the rotten egg smell? Does this not harm fish or microbes? It will harm them if there is too much of it, but it is normally not a problem. It does become more of a problem in winter when the ice prevents exchange of gases with the air. Keep in mind that anaerobic decomposition is a natural process that occurs at the bottom of all native ponds, where no one removes the leaves and muck.

As plants grow, they take up nutrients from water. Many of these plants are perennial, which die back in fall, and all of their leaves drop into the water. For some plants like cattails, the old leaves stay standing all winter. It is best to cut off this material and keep it out of the water, reducing the amount of nutrients in the water for next year.

Winter Care

Ponds in zone 7 or warmer rarely freeze over to any extent, and winter care is the same as summer care—you have nothing to worry about. There are special considerations for areas where the weather is cold enough to freeze the surface solid for two weeks at a time. Provided you select hardy plants, they will survive the winter with no extra care. Special winter care instructions for non-hardy plants are described in the chapter about plants.

Most fish can survive in a pond provided it does not freeze solid. Water cannot get any colder than 32°F without freezing. So even in sub-zero temperatures, the fish are at 32°F or warmer. But fish can suffer when the pond is covered with a solid piece of ice because it prevents the exchange of oxygen and CO_2 at the surface of the water. With an ice cap on the water, the oxygen level decreases while the CO_2 level increases, and the fish can suffocate. Most fish deaths in a pond are due to a lack of oxygen, not cold temperatures.

The easiest solution is to keep the surface of the water from freezing solid. The goal is to have at least a small opening in the ice for the gases to exchange with air. This can be done in two ways. Moving water does not freeze as easily as standing water. One way to keep it moving is to add an air pump and bubbling stone. These common supplies are sold at pet stores. Just place the air line into the water and anchor the air stone so it is below the surface of the water. Run the pump continuously during the cold parts of winter. The air pump works fine in zone 5, unless we get really cold temperatures for two consecutive weeks. Even with a bubbler going, the surface can freeze over.

A second option is to get a pond deicer or heater from pond supply houses, or you can make your own. (Some DIY solutions are included in the References section.) They float and keep the water around the heater warm enough so that it does not freeze. As long as the ice is not frozen solid, CO_2 and oxygen will exchange with the air and keep oxygen levels in the pond high enough for your fish.

The bubbler and heater can be combined to give even more protection. They don't need to be in the pond all winter, only when very low temperatures last for several days or a week. In zone 5, that is normally a six-week period.

Even if you don't have fish, you might think about keeping the surface of the pond open all winter. Frogs, who overwinter in your pond, have the same breathing problems as the fish.

Pond Leaks

The pond owner's worst fear is getting a leak in the liner. The good news is that if you use the recommended rubber pond liner and you followed the construction recommendations in this book, this is very unlikely. Most so-called leaks in a lined pond are due to water flowing over the edge of the liner, not holes in the liner. This is a bigger problem with streams and waterfalls because water runs near the top of the liner. Ponds are normally designed so the excess water only flows out the spillway and never gets near the edge of the liner except at the spillway.

How do you know you have a leak? It may not be obvious if the leak is small. The water level will drop a bit faster than normal. But what is normal? If you get a week of hot, windy weather, evaporation will be higher and the level will drop faster than normal. It always drops faster in mid-summer. So there really is no normal. It is something you will get a feel for over time.

Before a leak occurs, you can measure your evaporation rate. Put a mark on a stone or on a dock post. Make another mark a week later and measure the difference between the lines. You then know how fast the water level drops at that time of year. Record that number for future use.

If you think there's a leak, you should first go around the perimeter of the pond and make sure the edge of the liner has not slipped down below the water level. If it has, pull it back in place and support it with rocks or soil. You have solved the problem.

If that did not help, drop the water level so it is definitely below the spillway. If water is no longer leaking out, then you have a problem at the spillway or somewhere around the outside of the pond above the current waterline. Since the leak stopped when you dropped the waterline, you know the leak is now above that. Check to see that water is not running under the liner at the spillway. If the spillway is OK, then check around the outside of the pond for a leak above the current waterline.

If you still have not found the problem, there are two ways to proceed: a slow way and a fast way. The slow process is easier, but slower. You just wait until the water level starts dropping at the normal speed. When it reaches this point, you know that the leak is just above the current water level. Check all the way around the pond right at the water level. You are looking for a hole. A larger one made by animals will be easy to see; a smaller one can be difficult to find.

A quicker way to find the hole is to drop the water level one foot and see if you are losing water. If you are, drop the level another foot. Keep repeating this until you stop losing water. At that point, you know that the hole is somewhere in the foot above the current waterline. Check all the way around the pond until you find the hole.

In order to see a hole in the liner, you will have to remove any stones or protective material hiding the liner. That is a lot of work, and it is why I recommend adding a protective layer both above and below the liner and why you should only use the best rubber liner for the job. A well-constructed pond is not likely to have a hole.

Finding the hole in a pond liner is the hard part. Fixing it is easy and can be done without removing the liner from the pond. Obtain a pond liner repair kit and follow the instructions, similar to repairing a punctured bicycle tire. Once it is dry and sealed, you can refill the pond. The patch should outlive the rest of the liner.

CHAPTER 9

Large-scale Ponds

Large ponds are very similar to smaller backyard ponds, but they do require some special consideration. Most of the topics in this book apply to large ponds, but this chapter will focus on topics that are specific to large ponds.

Various names have been used for large ponds, including earth-lined ponds, earthen ponds, recreational ponds, fish ponds, and irrigation ponds. Design and construction for all are the same. For brevity, these will all be called ponds.

Special Pond Types

Large ponds can be used strictly for pleasure and aesthetics just like smaller backyard ones. But many times they are created to meet a special functional need. In that case, special design considerations might apply. The following are some typical pond applications. More than one of these may apply to your situation.

Irrigation Ponds

An irrigation pond is a great asset for farms of all types and sizes. It provides a ready source of water for crops and livestock. Most irrigation ponds are designed with steeper sides that don't have planting shelves. Because algae growth is not really a concern, plants don't play a critical role. Floating planktonic algae is not as big a problem since it will pump easily and add extra nutrients for plants. Filamentous algae tend to be less problematic since the water level is usually dropping during the season.

The main requirement for an irrigation pond is to hold lots of water, and the best way to do this is to make it as deep as possible. A deep pond loses relatively less water than a shallow pond since water only evaporates from the surface. A smaller surface means less water loss.

FIGURE 37
Farm ponds can be used for irrigation and watering livestock.

The location of an irrigation pond is usually determined by how it will be used. When the water is as close as possible to where it is needed, pumping is easier. Having electricity nearby can also be a big advantage.

Aquaculture Ponds

Having your own fish farm can be a great addition to a small farm. Smaller ponds provide food for your own use, and larger ponds will produce enough fish for sale. Aquaculture ponds should be at least one-quarter of an acre if you will be selling the fish.

The pond shown in figure 38 has a natural clay soil liner. It is built on top of a spring, which provides a steady source of cold fresh water. A shallow warmer end of the pond is used for swimming, and the deeper end near the spring provides the cold water needed for raising a small number of trout.

Ponds for raising fish are not very different from natural ponds. Plants are still important for keeping water clean and providing food for some types of fish.

FIGURE 38
Large pond used for swimming and raising trout.

A shallow pond heats up in summer, which can be very detrimental to some fish like trout. Therefore, most fish ponds are between 6 and 100 feet deep and may have several areas of different depths for various species. Research which ones you want to grow and then plan the depth to provide the right temperature conditions.

Many people try to grow a lot of fish in the pond to maximize productivity; this causes problems in a natural pond. To compensate, you may need pumps to aerate the water and keep oxygen levels high.

Think about how you will catch the fish. Will you go fishing with line and hook for the occasional meal, or do you want to harvest a large catch at the end of the season? To accomplish the latter, you will need to draw down the water and then have some type of net system to catch them.

The inflow and outflow systems should be constructed so that fish can't escape the pond; maybe include a net or grill system in these areas.

The key to maintaining a natural pond and raising fish is to keep fish levels reasonable. If these get too high, algae will become a problem.

Livestock Ponds

Ponds can be convenient ways to water livestock, both animals and waterfowl. If animals will be entering them to get a drink, provide a beach area for easier access.

Ponds can also be used to raise waterfowl for food or down. They prefer water between one-half foot and three feet deep and like to eat plants, so plan for larger planting areas. Good choices for geese and ducks include sago pondweed, wild celery, coontail, elodea, muskgrass, arrowhead, wild Japanese millet, and wild rice.

Wild animals such as coyotes like to eat large birds, so the pond may need protective fencing. An island for nesting ducks is another way to provide protection. In a larger pond, an island might even attract wild ducks or geese.

If animals or birds will use the water in winter, some of the surface should be kept open all winter long. Use solar-powered aerators for this.

Geothermal Ponds

Ponds can be used to provide a very economical way to heat and cool a home. Geothermal systems extract heat from the water in winter when the water temperature is 32°F. In summer, the cool water is used to extract heat from the home.

Pipes run from the home to the pond, where loops run under the water. A heat exchange fluid is pumped through the pipes from the home to the pond and back again. Heat exchangers inside the home transfer heat as needed and in turn warm or cool the air in the house. Such a geothermal system requires a pond that can maintain a depth of at least six feet.

Recreational Ponds

Recreational ponds for swimming have always been popular. They are very similar to most of the ponds described above, which can also be used for swimming.

How will swimmers enter and exit the water? One way would be by a dock, which could overcome steep slopes found in most ponds. Another is to add a large beach area, which should have a slope of no more than 4:1; less is better.

Locate beaches at the north end so bathers face south to make the best use of sunlight. It is best to keep it away from the inflow area, which tends to be murky and colder. Dig out the beach area six inches deep, line it with plastic, and then cover it with a layer of sand. Extend the beach above the high waterline to make it easy to enter the water.

Regulations and Permits

Ponds made in natural streams are highly regulated and may not be allowed in some areas. Be very careful about changing natural water flows.

Many rural landowners don't realize that they don't own the water that flows across their property. In the US, most lakes, wetlands, rivers, and streams belong to the government. Doing anything that impacts these waters requires permission from the EPA under the Clean Water Act. Any water that is not covered under federal jurisdiction is often covered under state laws.

A project that involves the building of a dam or embankment may increase your liability for any damage that happens downstream of your location. Contact your insurance provider to see if building a pond changes your policy.

Here are some agencies you should contact.

In the US:

- Natural Resources Conservation Service (NRCS): is part of the Department of Agriculture.
- County Conservation District (CCD): provides information about soil erosion and earth-moving activities.
- United States Army Corps of Engineers (USACE): is responsible for permits influenced by the Clean Water Act dealing with wetlands.
- State Department of Environmental Protection: is the state agency charged with water quality and quantity regulations.
- Local Fish and Boat Commission: regulates chemicals used in ponds and controls fish movement and addition to ponds.
- Local government (county, township, municipal): may have regulations and codes that affect the building of a pond.

In Canada:

- Ministry of Natural Resources: regulates natural creeks, streams, and wetlands.
- Local Conservation Authority: regulates local waterways.
- Ministry of Environment and Energy: requires permits when water comes from a natural watercourse at a rate exceeding 10,000 gallons a day, and for the use of herbicides to control aquatic vegetation.
- Local government (city, county, township, municipal): may have regulations and codes that affect the building of a pond.

Water Sources

Adding water to a large pond becomes an important consideration for its location. The best site may be where nature fills the pond for you and where you have to move the least amount of soil to get water. There are several possible water sources, and a combination of may be the best option, including the following.

Well Water

A special well can be dug near the pond location and equipped with a solar pump so that no electrical supply is required. Small pumps are also available for windmills. They require a wind of at least five miles per hour, which is less than what windmills require to generate electricity.

Well water is a good source but is generally only practical for smaller ponds or for topping up ponds that have another water source. Water witching, the process of using a forked stick to find water, is very popular, but this method does not work.

Surface Runoff

A good option is to position the pond where nature will supply most of the water. The base of a sloped hill can collect significant runoff. This hill should not be heavily fertilized, so that runoff does not add excess nutrients to the pond. Runoff from crop lands can add pesticides to the pond, and amphibians, in particular, are very sensitive to such chemicals.

Springs

A spring can be an excellent source of water. Most people try to locate the pond on top of it, but downstream from the spring is better because the rock around a spring can have high seepage rates. This will give you better control over the water flowing into the pond.

A pond liner can't be used on top of a spring since the water pressure from the spring will force it off the bottom of the pond.

Streams

Tapping into an existing stream or river is also possible, but this is highly regulated since it might affect living organisms in the stream. It is unlikely you will get a permit to build the pond right in the stream, but you might be able to divert a portion of it into your pond.

Liner Options

Large ponds can be made with the same rubber liner that is suggested for small ponds by joining pieces together to form the right size. There are other options that are worth considering.

The soil may hold water well enough to use it as a natural liner. A high water table will also help. Soil can be used if it contains at least 20 percent clay. Such earth-lined ponds always lose some water, which is called seepage. Soil with higher clay amounts seep less. A newly created pond seeps more in the first few years and becomes better sealed over time.

To find out how much clay is in your soil, dig some pilot holes to one foot below the planned depth of the pond. Collect the soil below the pond and determine the clay content. You can do this by sending samples to a soil lab, or using some DIY techniques to get a good approximation. The References section contains some links to YouTube videos on this process.

It is best to dig the pilot holes in summer or fall before fall rains start, so that you can see the natural low water level at that time of year. When digging, watch for horizontal rock ledges that can run long distances through soil and are a major cause of seepage, as the water runs along the rock. While you are testing the soil, you can also fill the pilot holes with water and monitor how quickly you lose water.

If the clay content is too low, bring in some good clay soil and line the pond to a depth of one foot, spread evenly and compacted to make a good seal. It should contain enough moisture so that it compacts well. Once it is laid, fill with water before the clay dries out and cracks. If you choose this option, it is probably best to hire an expert to do this work properly.

Instead of natural clay, you can also line the pond with a commercial product called bentonite, a colloidal clay that is applied to a dry pond bed. It works best on coarse-grained soil with low clay content. The bentonite is mixed into the native soil to a depth of four inches and then compacted. As water is added, it expands and forms a seal on the bottom of the pond. This is also a job best left to professionals who are familiar with the product and process.

Bentonite can also be used to fix holes in a natural soil pond if only a small section of the pond needs to be treated.

Cheaper plastic or PVC liners can also be used for large ponds. Since the plastic is easily damaged, it is usually covered with soil to protect it.

General Construction Considerations

There are two basic designs for large ponds: excavated and embankment. Figure 15 (page 57) shows the difference between these two types.

Excavated ponds, made by removing the soil, can be made on level or sloped ground. Their advantage is that there is no worry about edges of the pond collapsing. The downside of excavated ponds is that you need to dispose of a lot of soil.

Embankment ponds use the soil that is dug out to form part of the edge. They are usually built on sloped land where one end of the pond butts up against the hill. The removed soil is placed at the low end of the pond to raise up the edge. If it is sited well, this type requires less digging and there is no soil to remove. The downside of embankment ponds is that the dam needs to be constructed properly or it will collapse, sending all of the water flowing downhill. Build embankment ponds in an area where a breach of the dam will not flood homes or livestock.

Important notice: Always consult with a qualified professional engineer when designing and building an embankment pond or dammed pond. The author of this book is not an engineer and is not qualified to provide such consulting services.

The slope of the pond depends on both its type and use. An excavated pond that is used mostly for recreation or as a water source should have an inside slope of at least 2:1 (horizontal:vertical). An embankment pond should have a slope of 3:1 on the dam side. Beach areas where swimmers or livestock will be entering the water should be at least 4:1. Flatter slopes are more stable and will encourage algae and plant growth along the edge.

Except in beach areas, do not to put sand on the bottom. It discourages weeds for a while, but soon it will be covered with silt and you lose any benefits the sand gives.

The depth of the pond depends on its purpose. A deep pond loses less water to evaporation, which is good if you use it for irrigation. Increasing the depth is even more beneficial in warm dry locations with high evaporation rates. Deep water also stays cooler, which may be a requirement for raising some fish species. Less light gets to the bottom of a deep pond, making it harder for algae to grow. Shallower water is better when the pond is a wildlife refuge, since it can accommodate more plants.

> The volume of large ponds is usually expressed in terms of acre-feet, where 1 acre-foot is equal to 325,851 US gallons. The acre-foot of a pond is calculated as:
>
> Acre-foot = surface area (in acres) x average depth (in feet)

Aerators and Fountains

Aerobic decomposition (decomposition in the presence of oxygen) is favored in ponds because it is usually faster and free from offensive odors that characterize anaerobic decomposition. Pond aeration is used to increase the dissolved oxygen level so that aerobic decomposition can take place more efficiently. This is especially critical at the bottom of the pond where organic matter settles. An increased oxygen level can also be beneficial to fish.

Pond water will naturally separate into layers, or strata, through a process called stratification. This is mainly caused by temperature differences: warm water stays at the top, and cold water stays at the bottom. You have probably noticed this while swimming in a calm lake. Each layer of water also contains different amounts of oxygen: the top has the most oxygen, the bottom the least.

Aeration systems, designed to mix up these strata and increase the oxygen levels throughout the pond, do this by producing bubbles at the bottom that then rise to the surface. These bubbles only add a small amount of oxygen. Their main purpose is to lift cold water from the bot-

FIGURE 39
Solar-powered
aeration system.

tom to the surface, mixing up the strata. Oxygen from the air can then dissolve in the top water layer.

Fountains, often added for aesthetic reasons, can also be used to add oxygen to the water. As water from the spray hits the surface of the pond, it has the same effect as wind. It increases the rate at which gases exchange at the surface, thereby increasing oxygen levels. If the fountain gets its water from the bottom of the pond, it also helps to destratify the water layers.

Fountains are less expensive than aeration systems, but they are also less efficient at moving water. The inlet side of the pump also tends to clog, adding more maintenance work. They are better at moving duckweed to the edge of the pond than aeration systems.

Aeration systems and fountains can be solar-powered using commercial products or by making your own. The References section has some links to videos for making these systems.

Constructing Dams

To retain water, embankment ponds use a dam, which must be constructed with care and meet all regulations. This is not a beginner sport, and if you have never built a dam, you should get some expert advice. The recommendations presented in this book are just approximations. Requirements change depending on location, type of soil, and weather conditions. Check with local authorities to get the best dimensions for your situation.

Building a dam requires a lot of soil and could be the most expensive part of the project. The soil should be composed of high-quality clay containing very little organic matter, since that will decompose over time and shrink the soil level.

Add the soil in thin layers of no more than six inches at a time, compacting between layers. When complete, the inside slope should be at least 3:1 (horizontal:vertical) and the outside slope should be 4:1. Figure 40 shows a typical dam design.

The width of the top of the dam depends on its height. If less than 10 feet, then the dam should be 8 feet wide; if more than 10 feet, make the dam 12 feet wide. Wider dams are safer and easier to maintain. Dams that will be used as a road should be at least 16 feet wide.

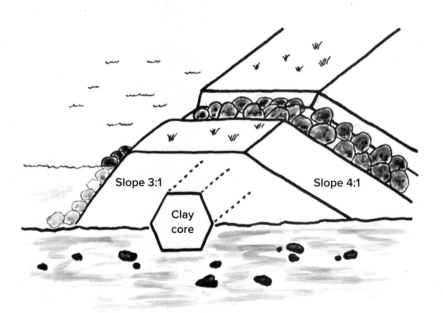

FIGURE 40
Dam for a large pond.

The center of the dam in figure 40 has a clay core, which can be added to large dams for extra stability. Speak to a dam specialist about adding this.

Plant the slopes of the dam as soon as possible to reduce erosion.

You will need to empty the pond occasionally to collect fish, perform maintenance, or clean it out. Drawing down some of the water can also reduce algae growth. You can add a drain system in the dam for emptying the pond, but these are the single largest cause for leakage. It is much better to empty the pond using pumps when needed. This may be slower and inconvenient, but it is less problematic. Drain systems are also more expensive to add.

Designing the Inflow

The pond should have a properly designed inflow area if it is being fed from a spring or river. It can also be a good way to control the water from surface runoff. An inflow is added to control erosion of soil beside the pond and to reduce the amount of silt entering the pond.

Erosion on the inflow usually occurs in spring as snow melts or in fall with heavy rains. Whenever a significant amount of water enters the pond, the inflow will tend to be eroded and the soil that is moved will flow into the pond. The best way to stop erosion in the inlet is to use rocks that are large enough so that the water cannot move them. Smaller rocks can then be added to fill the spaces between them. Use a rubber liner in the inlet area to further reduce damage to the inlet.

Figure 41 shows an inflow for a new pond that is made entirely out of concrete with a few stones added to slow down the movement of water.

Moving water carries silt, which on entering a pond will not only fill it up over time but also adds excess nutrients which increase algae problems. The recommended course of action is to design the inflow so that silt gets trapped before it enters the pond.

The best way to control silt is to add a small sediment pond ahead of the main pond. As the moving water enters the sediment pond, it slows down and the silt settles out of the water. The cleaner water can

FIGURE 41
Concrete inflow
on a new pond.

then be allowed to gently flow into the main pond. The silt that settles in the sediment pond can be emptied out periodically to keep the system working properly. The size of the sediment pond depends on how much and how fast the water is flowing into the system. Higher flow rates carry more silt than slower rates.

If a natural constant source of water flows into the main pond, consider raising the inflow above the waterline to create a waterfall. This adds an interesting architectural feature and helps aerate the water in the pond.

The inflow needs to be checked routinely, especially in early spring, to make sure the pathway for the water has not been plugged by vegetation or downed trees.

Designing the Outflow

The outflow on a pond is the area where excess water leaves the pond. If the pond is being fed by a stream or other constant flow of water, the outflow will serve this purpose. If the pond has no natural water source, the outflow is still required as an emergency system. If for some reason too much water enters the pond, the outflow provides a controlled method for dealing with the excess water, ensuring that it does not disrupt the dam.

The easiest way to construct the outflow is to create a rock-lined creek bed. The edge at the pond should be at the level needed to maintain its correct high-water level. The creek should then slope very gently away from the pond so that the water moves slowly. Stones added below the water level on the pond side of the outlet will help prevent erosion of the water side of the outflow.

The creek needs to be wide enough to easily handle the worst-case flooding situation. An approximate size can be calculated by adding 15 feet

FIGURE 42
Concrete dam
with outflow.

to one-half of the total drainage area (land and water collecting rain), in acres. For example, a 1-acre drainage area should be 16 feet wide, and a 5-acre area requires 17.5 feet.

A more elaborate outflow can be constructed to also help with emptying the pond. This requires the addition of a sluice gate and concrete support structures. It is best to consult a specialist for this project.

Plants

Planting a large pond is not much different than planting a smaller one, except that many more plants are needed. Types and quantity depends on the planned use of the pond. A wildlife refuge will normally have many more plants. A pond used to raise fish or for swimming needs to have more open water.

Shoreline Plants

Planting excavated ponds is fairly easy because you can choose anything you want. Combine shrubs and trees with herbaceous plants in any combination that suits your needs. Planting embankment ponds is a bit more challenging.

Trees and large shrubs should not be planted on the dam of an embankment pond. The tree roots will grow toward water sources such as the pond. In time they create weak points on the dam that increase water seepage. Small shrubs and grasses on the dam provide very good erosion control while still offering hiding places for wildlife. On new dams, use seed for annuals or perennials so that the bank is covered with some type of growth quickly to reduce erosion. Once this is established, other types of plants can be added.

Water Plants

A large pond can be designed with very distinct plant communities, and each area can be designed to have the best depth for the plants that will be grown there. The planting shelves in ponds that use a soil or clay liner will consist of the same soil that is used to line the bottom.

Plants are then rooted right into this soil. Don't add stones for plants on the shelf.

I recommend you cover half of the open water with floating plants like water lilies, which shade the water and make it more difficult for algae to grow. With less light in deep ponds, they stay colder, both of which discourages algae growth.

Eutrophication

Eutrophication is a term used to describe the aging process of a natural pond. Over time, sediment accumulates and reduces the depth of the pond. The amount of plants increases, which in turn reduces oxygen levels. The pond slowly becomes a swamp or wetland. You will need to decide on how much of this process you will allow.

CHAPTER 10

Pools, Bogs, and Rain Gardens

So far this book has discussed ponds as if they were isolated entities in the landscape. This chapter expands the idea of a pond to include other water features that you could build as stand-alone features in your landscape, but there are good reasons for combining them with a pond. For example, you could have a pool and a pond in two separate parts of your yard, but there are advantages for combining them in one spot.

Each feature is described as a separate entity, but in fact all of them could be combined into one large water feature. That would make for a very special pond.

Natural Swimming Pools

When people talk about swimming pools, they are normally talking about isolated water containers that are used only for swimming. In this book, the term pool refers to a natural swimming pool that is part of the pond.

Natural pools are popular in Europe, and are becoming more popular in North America. Usually part of a lined pond, these pools use no chemicals to disinfect the water and require no pump or filtration system, which makes them easier and cheaper to install and maintain.

Credit: David Pagan Butler, Organic Pools, by permission.

FIGURE 43
Natural swimming
pool designed by
Organic Pools.

The water feature is usually divided into two sections: the pond section for plants and the swimming area. Figure 43 shows such a water feature designed by David Pagan Butler. The dock leads down to a rectangular opening, which is the swimming area. Around the perimeter, the shallow pond consists mostly of planting shelves. The water flows freely between the two areas. David's website, listed in the References, offers a free e-manual on how to construct such a pool.

The idea of swimming in unchlorinated water might concern you, but consider that people have been swimming in lakes for a long time. This pool is really no different except that it is man-made.

The topics discussed in this book for keeping water in ponds clean also apply to these pools. Plants remove nutrients from the water and prevent algae from growing. Swimmers will contribute some organic matter like sweat, but the bacteria in the water will quickly degrade this into plant nutrients. The microbes and plants keep the water clean.

Construction techniques discussed in this book also apply to building natural pools. The following special issues may be relevant when planning this type of water feature.

Regulations

Many cities and counties have different bylaws and regulations for ponds and pools. In my town, a pond does not need to be fenced in, but a pool does. What is the difference? It is the intent that matters. If the water feature is built for swimmers, it is a pool and needs a fence. Make sure you check with local authorities to understand the required regulations in your area.

Size

Most backyard ponds tend to be too small for swimming. If your goal is to create a pool that your family can use for swimming, it needs to be larger. Remember that one-third to one-half of the surface are will be used for plants. Figure out how much room you want for swimming and double the area for the complete pond.

Swimming with Fish

One concern people have with a natural pool is that they would be swimming with the wildlife, things like tadpoles, frogs, and insects. To some extent, this is true, but most of the wildlife prefers to live in the shallow water with the plants. Frogs and insects will tend to stay away from the deeper swimming area. This is one reason to keep the plants and swimming area separate.

If you choose to add fish, they will usually hide when swimmers arrive. But even if they don't, they won't hurt swimmers any more than the natural fish in lakes do.

Safety

Are natural pools safe? Other than possible issues with drowning, the other concern about natural pools is bacterial contamination. The reason chlorine is added to most pools is to kill bacteria so they won't infect humans. Without chlorine is there a concern about bacterial contamination? Testing has shown the most natural pools in Europe are safe. The amount of bacterial contamination is low, probably a result of birds visiting the area.

Muddy Bottoms

If you follow the recommended construction techniques, the bottom of the pond will be a rubber liner. This is not much different than the liners used in conventional pools. It feels like plastic or rubber on your feet, and tends to be slippery. If the water is too deep for you to stand on the bottom, it's never a problem. For shallower ponds, you can add a layer of sand on the bottom, right on the liner, to give the pool a more natural feel on the feet. The sand is not coarse enough to cause a puncture, even with people standing on it.

Stagnant Water

In a natural pond, the wind is strong enough to move the water around and keep it from becoming stagnant. A natural pool tends to be deeper and have a larger open water area. Wind will still circulate the water but not as effectively.

When constructing a natural pool, it is worth considering some method for increasing water circulation. This will keep the water cleaner and warm up the swimming area by moving the shallow warm water around plants into the deep colder water.

Extra circulation can be added in a number of ways. One simple way is to add a bubbler system as discussed in the chapter on large ponds. This can be a solar system that creates bubbles in the bottom of the pool and moves the cold water to the surface. The bubbles oxygenate and circulate the water.

A pumping system can also be added to take water from the deep end of the pool and pump it into the far side of the planting section. The pumped water then flows through the plants where it is cleaned and warmed up. In a normal pool, this pumping system is usually large and underground, making the whole thing much more complicated than necessary. You can simply have hoses hidden under rocks along the edge of the pond going from one end to the other end of the pool. They can be removed in winter if freezing is a concern.

The pump can be located at the far end so that swimmers will not hear or see the pump. It can be powered by line voltage or solar panel. This system can be made more efficient by replacing the normal planting shelves with a bog filter, as described below. The water then flows up through the gravel and across the top of planting stones into the swimming area. This cleans the water more efficiently but is a bit more complicated to install.

Maintenance

The maintenance of a natural pool is about the same as for a natural pond. In a pond, you don't worry about the accumulation of organic matter in the bottom, but in a pool, you will probably want to clean this out periodically so that swimmers' feet are not walking on the muck. Use a vacuum pump or a simple fish net.

In the fall, cut back vegetation to keep it from accumulating in the bottom of the pool. Other than trying to keep the water a bit cleaner than in a pond, the maintenance is really the same. You don't need to add chemicals or adjust pH or ammonium levels. Water needs to be topped up from time to time. There is no special winter maintenance required; just let the pool freeze over. Some people even use the pool as a skating rink in winter.

Entering the Pool

A pool should have an easy way for swimmers to enter and leave it. A larger beach will work, but they usually take up precious swimming room.

Many people add a dock and steps into the pool as shown in figure 43. It can be made from wood to maintain the more natural feel of the pool.

Bogs

The word "bog" creates an image of a shallow, weedy, bug-infested water feature that smells. Why would anyone want this near a pond?

A bog can also be a special type of garden that stays wet or at least moist most of the year. It does not have to have standing water in it. This form of bog can be used to grow some very interesting plants that will not flourish in normal garden beds because they are too dry. So a bog is a new type of gardening.

Bogs also work well with ponds, since the overflow of the pond needs to go somewhere. It might as well go into a special garden bed that con-

FIGURE 44
Building a bog. Hole is dug and lined with plastic, before being refilled with soil.

tains plants that like to be wet. On level ground, I always add a bog at the overflow area of the pond.

The bog is built in much the same way as a pond. You start by digging a hole that is about 18 inches deep. Don't worry about the slope of the sides because it will be filled with soil again.

The shape and size of the bog can be anything you want. Once the bog is finished, you will hardly see the edges, so the shape is not critical. Size does not affect functionality. Design it for aesthetic reasons.

Line the bottom and sides of the hole with plastic. This does not have to be expensive pond liner. You can use cheap clear plastic vapor barrier that is used for building homes. The thicker variety is easier to use. Lay it in the hole so that some excess comes up the sides of the hole and over the edge.

This type of man-made bog does not hold water, so you must poke holes or make slits with a utility knife in the bottom of the plastic. The number is not critical, but add enough so that if one gets plugged with soil, the others can drain. I realize those instructions are not very helpful, but I've made several bogs with different size and number of holes and they all work.

Fill the bog with the soil you removed. Bog plants like soil containing lots of organic matter, so you can amend it with materials like peat moss or compost. If you do add organic matter, place all of the original soil plus the amendment back into the hole. The organic matter decomposes over time, and the soil level will settle back at the right level.

Trim off the excess plastic about an inch below grade so you can't see any of it. If the bog is part of another garden bed, place some marker stones along the edge of the bog. If you don't do this, in two years you won't remember where the edge is.

Plant the bog in the same way you would plant any other garden bed. Then water your new plants and add mulch on top of the soil.

How does the bog work? When water is added to the bog, it will run through the soil until it reaches the plastic. It then settles there and only slowly runs past the plastic through the holes you made. The plastic layer acts like a big diaper keeping the soil wet. The mulch on top of the soil reduces evaporation into the air. As a result, the bog stays wet for a long time.

I built one of my first bogs in full sun. Without any runoff water from a pond, the soil in it stays moist all summer long without any additional watering. In comparison, other normal garden beds need to be watered a few times throughout the summer, even though they are mulched. The wettest part of my garden, the bog, never seems to dry out. The bog is a great place to plant all kinds of perennials that like constant moisture at their roots.

Bog Filters

A bog filter is a special kind of bog that is used to filter and clean the water from ponds and pools. In a pool, it can be the exclusive filtering system, or it can be combined with plants growing in the pool area. A bog filter is also used in conjunction with ponds and waterfalls for additional filtration in the system.

There are many ways to construct the bog filter, and I will only provide some general design information here. The bog system consists of four main components: bog, filtration media, plumbing, and plants.

The bog itself is constructed just like a small pond using a rubber liner. The size depends on the amount of water you want to filter and

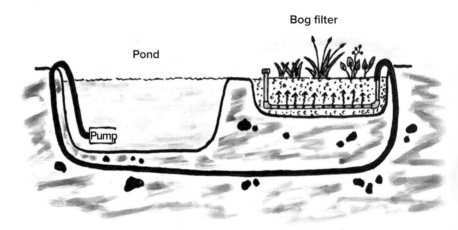

FIGURE 45
Bog filter and pond.

the space available. A larger system provides more filtration. If you are using this for a pond or pool that does not contain plants, then it should be one-third to one-half the size of the main water feature. It is usually located near the water it is cleaning, but it can be further away. The depth should be at least 18 inches; 36 inches works better in zone 5 and colder areas, due to freezing.

The bog is filled with filtration media that can include sand and gravel. The material should be larger than the holes drilled in the plumbing, and it should be washed to get rid of fine particles. A good option is washed ⅜-inch pea gravel.

Plumbing, added at the bottom of the bog, consists of a manifold with a series of 1½-inch PVC pipe laid out much like a septic field. The main inlet is split into any number of parallel lines. Add one line for every two feet of bog width and run the lines the length of the bog. At the end of each line, add an elbow and a vertical piece of tubing that reaches two inches above the top level of the bog. The top is fitted with a male fitting and screw cap so that it can be opened for cleaning.

These vertical end pipes will allow you to flush the system should it get plugged. Simply remove the cap, and the pump will push water and collected debris out of the tube. You can also disconnect the inlet side and push a garden hose down the vertical end pipes to back flush the system.

The PVC pipe along the bottom of the bog is drilled with ¼-inch holes, every two inches. The holes should face up so they don't push water against the pond liner.

When water is pumped into the pipes, it exits the pipes at the bottom of the bog. This forces the water already in the bog to flow up through the filtration media until it gets to the top of bog. At that point, it will over flow the bog and run back into the pond or pool.

The return system to the pool can be done using pipes, or it can be a simple inlet as described in the chapter on building large ponds. If the bog is located uphill from the pool, then it can also flow into the pond as a waterfall, providing both clean water and aeration.

After construction, the bog is filled with plants that like having their roots growing in water, which includes all of the pond plants. Water lilies do not grow well in the bog filter.

The secret to the bog filter are the plants and microbes. The microbes will grow in the filter media, converting organic matter into nutrients that encourage plant growth.

The bog filter works quite well, but it does require the addition of a pump, which is not required for the natural ponds and pools discussed here. The advantage of the bog filter is that it removes the plants from the main pond or pool. For some, this makes the pool more inviting for swimming. The bog filter is also a good option for people who want to keep koi, which tend to eat plants.

Rain Gardens

A rain garden is a special kind of garden that is both a unique place to grow plants and a way of solving an environmental problem. It can be designed completely separate from a pond, or it can become an integral part of the pond, providing an extra source of water.

Every time it rains, water runs off roofs and driveways and usually runs into city storm water systems. The city then needs to clean and dispose of this. It is much better for the environment if this water remains on your property, and a rain garden can do this.

A rain garden is simply a depression in the landscape that is positioned to collect runoff. The water sits there until it seeps into the soil below it. One of the best sources of water for a rain garden is the downspouts on your home.

Instead of having the excess water sit in the rain garden, it can be directed towards the pond, providing a good source of water for topping it up. To make this work, position it higher than the pond, but lower than the grade around the house. That way all of the water flows easily without any pumping system. The slope should be at least one inch per ten feet; larger slopes work better.

If you are building a rain garden that is not connected to the pond, it is important to make it large enough to hold all of the excess water and to provide enough soil to accept the runoff. The requirement is different if you are connecting the rain garden to a pond. Instead of it holding all of the water, you want most of the water flowing through the rain garden into the pond so the size of the rain garden can be much smaller. In fact, it can be reduced so much that it looks more like a river leading down to the pond.

Start building the rain garden by digging the center so that it is 6 to 12 inches lower than the surrounding soil. A narrow rain garden with a gradual slope needs to be deeper to handle the water flow. A wide one or one that has a steeper slope can be shallower, since the water does not fill it up as quickly.

In areas with little rainfall, it is a good idea to line the center of the rain garden with plastic so more of the water gets to the pond before it soaks into the soil. If using plastic, you will probably want to dig the garden a bit deeper, and then cover the plastic with soil or rocks so that it is not visible. Where the plastic meets the edge of the pond, make sure you lay the plastic over the pond liner so the water does not run under it.

An inflow will need to be added at the point where the water runs into the pond. This is described more fully in the chapter on large ponds. Scale the size to match the size of your pond. The inflow into the pond should be higher than the spillway. This will ensure that an overflow of the pond will not back up into the rain garden. Instead it will flow out at the spillway and right into the bog garden, if you decided to add one.

Once the rain garden is complete, it can be planted with species that grow well in wet conditions. Make sure the size and design make it look like part of the natural landscape around the pond. When done correctly, nobody will know you have a rain garden, unless they recognize some of the plants that like wet feet.

References

Online group for discussing natural ponds, Facebook Group called
   "Building Natural Ponds":
   facebook.com/groups/buildingnaturalponds

Understand garden hardiness zones:
   gardenfundamentals.com/planting-zones-hardiness-zones

Free e-book about natural pools:
   organicpools.co.uk/DIY%20DVD.htm

YouTube video showing natural pools:
   youtube.com/watch?v=7JoQthEBl6U

Lots of pictures of natural pool designs:
   inspirationgreen.com/natural-pools-swimming-ponds.html

Cattail — how to prepare and eat every part of the plant:
   permacultureproject.com/plant-of-the-month-cattail-the-supermarket-of
   -the-swamp

DIY Solar powered aerators:
   youtube.com/watch?v=UyTTbt-dpRQ

Good discussion about ice freezing on ponds:
   lakeice.squarespace.com/ice-growth

Learn more about pond liners:
   graystonecreations.com/Firestone-Pondgard-45-Mil-EPDM-Pond-Liner
   _ep_60.html

Joining pieces of pond liners:
   pondexperts.ca/pond-advice-tips/join-epdm-rubber-pond-liner

DIY pond deicers:
   jennie_in_mt.tripod.com/deicerpop.html

Measuring clay content in soil:
  youtube.com/watch?v=AUhOBxVFcFk

More information about the author's ponds:
  gardenmyths.com/pond-pumps-filters

General gardening information:
  gardenfundamentals.com

Index

About the Author

ROBERT PAVLIS, a Master Gardener with 40 years of gardening experience, is owner and developer of Aspen Grove Gardens, a six-acre botanical garden featuring over 2,500 varieties of plants. A popular and well-respected speaker and teacher, Robert has published articles in *Mother Earth News*, *Ontario Gardening* magazine, a monthly *Plant of the Month* column for the Ontario Rock Garden Society website, and  local newspapers. He is also the author of widely read blog GardenMyths.com, which explodes common gardening myths, and GardenFundamentals.com, which provides gardening and garden design information.

Also by the Author

If you are enjoying this book you may also like my other book. *Garden Myths* examines over 120 horticultural urban legends. Turning wisdom on its head, Robert Pavlis dives deep into traditional garden advice and debunks the myths and misconceptions that abound. He asks critical questions and uses science-based information to understand plants and their environment. Armed with the truth, Robert then turns this knowledge into easy-to-follow advice. For more information and ordering details, visit: gardenmyths.com/garden-myths-book-1/

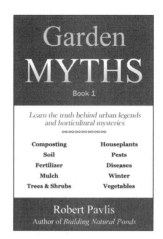

Are you interested in learning more about building ponds and water falls? Consider joining our Facebook Group: https://www.facebook.com/groups/buildingnaturalponds/

A Note About the Publisher

NEW SOCIETY PUBLISHERS (www.newsociety.com), is an activist, solutions-oriented publisher focused on publishing books for a world of change. Our books offer tips, tools, and insights from leading experts in sustainable building, homesteading, climate change, environment, conscientious commerce, renewable energy, and more—positive solutions for troubled times.

Sustainable Practices for Strong, Resilient Communities

We print all of our books and catalogues on 100% **post-consumer recycled paper**, processed chlorine-free, and printed with vegetable-based, low-VOC inks. These practices are measured through an Environmental Benefits statement (see below). We are committed to printing all of our books and catalogues in North America, not overseas. We also work to reduce our carbon footprint, and purchase carbon offsets based on an annual audit to ensure carbon neutrality.

Employee Trust and a Certified B Corp

In addition to an innovative employee shareholder agreement, we have also achieved B Corporation certification. We care deeply about *what* we publish—our overall list continues to be widely admired and respected for its timeliness and quality—but also about *how* we do business.

For further information, or to browse our full list of books and purchase securely, visit our website at: **www.newsociety.com**

New Society Publishers
ENVIRONMENTAL BENEFITS STATEMENT

For every 5,000 books printed, New Society saves the following resources:[1]

23	Trees
2,127	Pounds of Solid Waste
2,341	Gallons of Water
3,053	Kilowatt Hours of Electricity
3,867	Pounds of Greenhouse Gases
17	Pounds of HAPs, VOCs, and AOX Combined
6	Cubic Yards of Landfill Space

[1] Environmental benefits are calculated based on research done by the Environmental Defense Fund and other members of the Paper Task Force who study the environmental impacts of the paper industry.